THE NO-COOK COOKBOOK

by
Jayne Benkendorf

Published by
Ludwig Publishing
Edmond, OK

Library of Congress Cataloging-in-Publication Data

THE NO-COOK COOKBOOK
by Jayne Benkendorf
Includes Index.
ISBN: 0-9651990-3-7   99-64270
                                                                  CIP

THE NO-COOK COOKBOOK
by Jayne Benkendorf
Copyright 1999 by Jayne Benkendorf

Printed in the United States of America by:
RG Printing
706 W. California
Oklahoma City, OK 73102

Book cover design by: Tim Duncan, RG Printing, Oklahoma City, OK

Price: $14.95

DISCLAIMER:

It should be noted that in no way is any information contained herein to be construed
as a prescription or medical advice, or is this information in any way to preclude the
need or advice of a health professional. In fact, it is recommended that should you
wish to change your diet because of any information contained herein, you should
first consult a health professional, especially if you are currently taking medication
and/or have a physical impairment. All rights reserved. If you do not wish to be
bound by the above, you may return this book for a full refund to:

Meals In Minutes
P.O. Box 1828
Edmond, OK 73083-1828

TABLE OF CONTENTS

4

MY MESSAGE TO YOU

Hello Dear Reader,

I must tell you that I had **GREAT FUN** writing this cookbook. I never have enjoyed scrubbing pots and pans, so it was a treat to fix all these dishes and not have even one pot to wash!

You may want to fix these dishes because there is very little mess to clean up, or you may *have* to fix dishes that require no cooking because you don't have a source of heat. You may be out of electricity or gas for a variety of reasons; power failures, hurricanes, tornadoes, floods, earthquakes, etc. If you have your pantry stocked with ingredients for these dishes, you will have nutritious meals, snacks, etc. at your fingertips.

Many of these dishes are so simple a child can fix them. I would suggest getting your children involved in helping fix some of these recipes. Remember that when a child is involved in helping prepare food, he or she is much more likely to eat it. Preparing these dishes will teach them what to eat for good health, and it will also teach them to be self-sufficient.

Know that with these recipes, you will be feeding your family good, wholesome food.

Have fun, and enjoy!

In Good Health,

Jayne Benkendorf

INTRODUCTION

WHAT MAKES THIS COOKBOOK DIFFERENT...

Talk about simple to fix - these are it!!

No pots and pans to scrub!!

These meals, salads, desserts, etc. are not only simple to fix, they're *very* nutritious. Some dishes are vegetarian, and others contain some cheese or meat.

In my recipes, I use only whole grains - no refined flour and no refined sugar. You can feel good about serving these dishes to your family.

Only healthful ingredients are used, with no harmful additives or preservatives. You will notice that I recommend specific brands of food products in these recipes. These are products that are free of harmful additives and preservatives. If the brands I recommend are not available in your area, you may want to purchase *The Food Storage Bible* to help you make other choices in your stores. (For information about purchasing *The Food Storage Bible*, see page 158.)

Realize that you may not be familiar with certain brand names because they aren't highly advertised, yet they may very well be on your grocery shelves. Many healthful products can be found in the "diet" section of grocery stores. But know that just because a product is located in the diet section, this does not necessarily mean that it is healthful.

Most of these dishes provide abundant energy because of the high quality complex carbohydrates–whole grains and legumes (beans, peas, and lentils.)

Many dishes contain fresh fruits and vegetables. For good health, it is important to eat fresh fruits and vegetables daily. Five to nine servings are recommended. (When it comes to fresh produce, I think more is better!)

If you're in a situation where fresh food is not available, you can easily get the nutrients and active enzymes of fresh food by sprouting seeds. I think it is always a good idea to have sprouting seeds available in case there is a shortage of fresh fruits and vegetables.

If sprouting is new to you, I encourage you to give it a try. Sprouts are good any time, not just in emergency situations. Learn to sprout and enjoy the benefits now. To learn more about sprouting, see page 145.

You will have a satisfied feeling when you serve your family the nutritious dishes made from these recipes. And you'll also feel good because you don't have to scrub those pots and pans!

Have fun, and be healthy!

BEVERAGES

Water is always the best choice when it comes to beverages - BUT, many times we get tired of plain ol' water. On the next page is my favorite drink. I hope you try it. I think you'll like it.

GRAPE-CITRUS DRINK

Serves 1

> 1 glass ice
>
> 7/8 glass water
>
> 1/8 glass purple grape juice
>
> Wedge of lemon or lime

- Put ice and water in glass.
- Top off with grape juice.
- Squeeze lemon or lime into glass.
- Drop wedge in glass.

No need to stir. Just drink and enjoy!

You may want to use less water and more juice. I use just enough juice to flavor the water. The idea is to drink much more water than juice.

This drink is so refreshing, summer or winter. It's not only tasty, it has some great things going for it.

First, lemons and limes act as cleansing agents. They help rid the kidneys of toxins.

Second, purple (or red) grape juice contains the powerful antioxidant resveratrol. Resveratrol inhibits free radical formation and thus helps prevent cancerous tumors. It was also found that resveratrol can inhibit the progression of established cancer.[*]

What a tasty way to help prevent cancer!

[*] Jang, Meishiang, et. al., "Cancer Chemopreventive Activity of Resveratrol, a Natural Product Derived from Grapes", Science, 275, January 10, 1997, pg 218-220.

SPORTS DRINKS

Most sports drinks, including Gatorade, contain primarily sugar-water and artificial colors. There are very small amounts of potassium and sodium (electrolytes) added to these sports drinks.

What most people want in sports drinks are the electrolytes lost when they perspire. Well, Gatorade has only 110mg sodium and 30mg potassium. Not much at all!

There is a *much* better choice. In fact there are two good choices. We can make our own sports drinks by adding a bit of salt to fruit or veggie juices OR we can drink V8 Juice.

An 8oz glass (1 cup) of orange juice has 480mg of potassium and 25mg of sodium. By adding only 1/8 teaspoon salt, we add 290mg of extra sodium. Now, we have a wonderful sports drink with nutritious ingredients, no refined sugar or artificial colors!

How about V8 Juice? V8 is made from a variety of vegetables with no sugar or artificial colors. A 5.5oz can has 380mg of potassium and 430mg of sodium. What a simple, nutritious way to get electrolytes!

Let's look at juice choices and the milligrams of potassium in 8 ounces (1 cup):

JUICE	POTASSIUM
Grape	335
Pineapple	335
Grapefruit	374
V8	380
Orange-Grapefruit	390
Orange	480
Tomato	535
Prune	705

These truly are healthful choices for potassium. Now for a 'true' sports drink, add 1/8 teaspoon salt to each of these juices - except V8 Juice. (V8 already contains sodium.)

Remember that it's *very* important to drink plenty of water when participating in physical activities, particularly in hot weather. Drink. Drink. Drink water - even though you may not feel thirsty. Then occasionally have one of these good-for-you sports drinks.

If you like spicy drinks, you'll love this one!

SPICY MARY

Makes 4 cups

2 cups crushed ice

1 3/4 cup *Spicy Hot V8 Juice*

1 TB fresh lemon juice

1/4 tsp celery seed

1 cup firm or extra firm tofu

• Put all ingredients in blender; blend until smooth.

Pass the celery sticks!

Because of the Spicy Hot V8, this truly is spicy. If you like a milder drink, use regular V8 Juice.

* * *

Smoothies make marvelous tasting drinks that can be very healthful. For great smoothies, see page 15.

For a wonderful book that contains only nutritious smoothies, see *1-2-3 Smoothies* by Rita Bingham, page 160.

SMOOTHIES

Smoothies are very special, tasty drinks that are packed with nutrients. There is nothing better than a fruit-filled, icy drink on a hot summer day.

Many people have a protein drink or other type drink for breakfast. A fruit smoothie with a whole grain muffin would make a wonderful breakfast, packed with nutrients as well as active enzymes.

If you have never eaten tofu, but you have heard of its health benefits and think you'd like to give it a try, this smoothie is a great place to begin. You won't even know you're eating tofu!

BANANA - STRAWBERRY -TOFU SMOOTHIE

Makes 1 1/2 cups

> 3/4 cup firm or extra firm tofu
>
> 1 cup chunked fresh strawberries
>
> 1 medium frozen, ripe banana broken into pieces*
>
> 1 TB strawberry all-fruit jam *(Smuckers)*

- Put all ingredients in a blender; blend until smooth.

This is a *very* nutritious smoothie with the tofu and fruit. It is packed with a variety of nutrients, active enzymes, and even estrogen in the tofu. What a power-packed drink!

---

* To freeze bananas: Peel ripe bananas and space them on a baking sheet so they don't touch. Freeze. After they're frozen, put in a plastic bag and take one out as you need it. (Be sure to peel your bananas before freezing them. If you don't, you'll have a mess. I know. I did it - once!)

Soy milk is healthful, and it's especially good for those who are sensitive to dairy products. If you have never tried soy milk, in a smoothie would be a great place to start. You won't be able to tell that this smoothie contains soy milk.

BANANA - STRAWBERRY SOY MILK SMOOTHIE

Makes 1 serving

1 cup lowfat soy milk

1 frozen, ripe banana, broken into pieces*

5 large, fresh strawberries

2 TB apple juice concentrate

2 TB wheat germ

1/2 cup crushed ice

• Put all ingredients in a blender; blend until smooth.

This is another nutritious smoothie with the soy milk, fruit, and wheat germ. It is packed with a variety of nutrients, active enzymes, and even estrogen in the soy milk. What a power-packed drink!

* To freeze bananas, see page 16

Smoothies can be made with yogurt just as well as with milk, tofu, or soy milk. Most yogurt contains lactobacillus acidophilus. Acidophilus is a potent promoter of beneficial bacteria. Many times yogurt is recommended when a person has a yeast infection, after a course of antibiotics, and in case of diarrhea.

Many people who are lactose intolerant are able to eat yogurt since it contains 75% of the lactose found in milk.

BANANA - STRAWBERRY YOGURT SMOOTHIE

Makes 2 servings

1 cup plain, nonfat yogurt

1 cup fresh strawberries

1 large ripe banana

1/4 cup wheat germ

1/4 cup orange juice

1 cup crushed ice

1/2 tsp vanilla

- Put all ingredients in a blender; blend until smooth.

Feel free to use other fruits in smoothie drinks. Be creative.

Give these fruits a try:

Kiwi	Mango
Oranges	Pineapple
Raspberries	Blueberries
Blackberries	

Here's another great smoothie. I nearly always have these ingredients on hand to make this tasty drink.

BANANA SPARKLER

Makes 1 serving

1 cup skim milk*

1/4 cup apple juice concentrate**

1 frozen, ripe banana***

2 TB wheat germ

(Nutmeg, optional)

• Put all ingredients in a blender; blend until smooth.

* You may certainly substitute soy milk for the skim milk. You may also use firm or extra firm tofu, or plain, nonfat yogurt.

** You may use different juices such as pineapple juice or white grape juice. If you use white grape juice, look for brands that do not contain sulfites.

*** To freeze bananas, see page 16.

When you keep these ingredients on hand, you have a nutritious, tasty smoothie in very few minutes.

ORANGE - BANANA SMOOTHIE

Makes 2, one cup servings

    1/2 cup firm or extra firm tofu

    1/2 cup orange juice

    1 frozen, ripe banana*

    1 cup crushed ice

• Put all ingredients in a blender; blend until smooth.

This smoothie reminds me of a dreamsicle. Dreamsicles were one of my favorites as a child. But I know those weren't nearly as nutritious as this 'dreamsicle'!

* To freeze bananas, see page 16.

The flavor of this smoothie is superb! I love the combination of raspberries and bananas. See what you think.

RASPBERRY - BANANA SMOOTHIE

Makes 5 cups

1 pkg (12.3oz) *Mori-Nu Lite Tofu*, firm or extra firm

1 cup skim milk, or lowfat soy milk

2/3 cup *Dole Country Raspberry* frozen concentrate

2 frozen, ripe bananas

Crushed ice (about 2 cups)

• Put all ingredients in a blender; blend until smooth.

For other taste treats, use a variety of frozen fruit juice concentrates. Use only those without refined sugars, and without sulfites - in other words, just plain juice.

Your taste buds will love you for this one! This is truly a scrumptious smoothie. It tastes like pumpkin pie!

This recipe is from Rita Bingham's cookbook, *1-2-3 Smoothies*. To learn more about Rita's books, see pages 159 and 160.

If you're a fan of pumpkin pie, you're going to love this one! If you don't have the ingredients on hand for this smoothie, *run* to the store.

CREAMY PUMPKIN PIE

Makes 2 servings

1 cup low fat soy milk (or skim milk)

1/2 cup apple juice concentrate

1/3 cup canned pumpkin

1/4 tsp cinnamon

1/2 tsp vanilla

Dash nutmeg

1/2 frozen, ripe banana*

6 ice cubes, crushed

• Put all ingredients in blender; blend until smooth.

* To freeze bananas, see page 16.

SOUPS

When cooler weather approaches, soup sales soar. We can buy our soup, or we can make our own.

Have you ever tried cold soup on a hot day? It's wonderful!

I hope you give all these soups a try.

Since in this cookbook we don't use pots and pans, we'll fix this soup in a bowl. If you want hot soup, heat it on the stove.

BLACK BEAN SOUP

Makes 6 cups

2 cans (15oz each) black beans

1 can (14.5oz) chicken broth (*Swanson 1/3 Less Sodium*)

1 bunch green onions, chopped

3 garlic cloves, minced

1 1/2 tsp cumin

3/4 tsp oregano

- Put all ingredients in a bowl; mix well.

This is ready to eat as-is. Or put in mugs and heat in the microwave.

This soup is packed with energy (the black beans), fat is nonexistent, it's very tasty, and it's very quick to fix. What a deal!

SERVE WITH THIS:

Fat free sour cream*

Hot sauce (*Pace*)

Tortilla chips (For *Guiltless Gourmet Chips*, see page 73.)

Raw veggies such as, carrot sticks, cauliflower florets, etc.

With raw veggies, you now have a complete meal.

---

* Look for sour cream that does not contain potassium sorbate, artificial color, or artificial flavor.

I often wondered what tortilla soup tasted like, but I knew I didn't want all the fat that's usually in this soup. So, I came up with a recipe that has virtually no fat.

Not only is it missing all that fat, it's very quick and easy to fix - and it's *very* tasty.

TORTILLA SOUP

Makes 5 1/2 cups

1 small onion, chopped

2 cans (14.5oz each) chicken broth *(Swanson 1/3 Less Sodium)*

2 garlic cloves, minced

1 can (4oz) chopped green chilies

1 cup cooked chicken or turkey, chunked*

1 can (16oz) stewed tomatoes, drained

Corn tortillas *(Guiltless Gourmet, see page 73.)*

• Combine all ingredients in a large bowl - all but the chips.

Put the soup in mugs and eat as-is - or heat on the stove. Crumble corn chips into the soup.

This is a light soup that's great to serve before a Mexican meal. I think you'll enjoy it, particularly if you like Mexican flavor.

If you've never had cold cucumber soup, you've missed a great one.

This soup is pretty to look at and very refreshing to eat. I think you'll be surprised at how good cold cucumber soup can taste. I do hope you give this one a try.

CUCUMBER SOUP

Makes 3 1/2 cups

> 1 large cucumber (12oz) unpeeled, cut into 1/2 inch slices
>
> 1 container (8 oz) plain, nonfat yogurt
>
>   OR 3/4 pkg *Mori-Nu Lite Tofu,* firm or extra firm
>
> 1 cup chicken broth *(Swanson 1/3 Less Sodium)*
>
> 2 TB chopped onion
>
> 1 garlic clove
>
> 2 tsp dried dill weed
>
> 1/2 tsp salt
>
> Dash hot pepper sauce

• Put all ingredients in a food processor or blender. Blend until smooth and creamy.

Serve immediately or refrigerate for a "cool" cucumber soup.

Garnish each serving with a sprig of fresh dill or parsley or celery leaves.

This soup is truly delightful. It is so refreshing in summer when it is served chilled. I hope you enjoy it as much as my family does.

How about another wonderful cold soup for hot summer days? This is a *very* tasty and popular Spanish soup that is both nutritious and energy-packed.

GAZPACHO

Makes 4 large servings

1 pkg (10oz) frozen baby lima beans, thawed

3 medium tomatoes, chopped (about 2 cups)

1 medium red bell pepper, chopped (Use the seeds.)

1 small cucumber, chopped (1/2 cup)

3 green onions, chopped

1 garlic clove, minced

1 1/2 cups V8 vegetable juice

3 TBS vinegar

1 tsp dried dillweed

1/4 tsp salt

Several dashes Tabasco Sauce*

Fat free sour cream

• Put all ingredients in a large bowl. (All but the sour cream.)
• Stir well.
• Top each serving with a dollop of sour cream.

This soup is excellent served immediately, or it can be chilled to eat cold. Either way it is very good.

Pass the Guiltless Gourmet Tortilla Chips. (See page 73.)

---

* If you don't care for the hot, spicy taste of Tabasco, omit it.

This soup is soooo refreshing on a hot summer's day. Take advantage of the in-season fruits to make this cool, yummy, fruit soup.

CHILLED FRUIT SOUP

Makes 5 servings

2 cups cantaloupe pieces
4 cups honeydew pieces
2 cups mango pieces
1 cup fresh orange juice
1/4 cup fresh lime juice
1 cup firm or extra firm tofu
2 TB apple juice concentrate

Fresh strawberries

- Chill all ingredients.
- Reserve 1/2 cup cantaloupe, 1/2 cup honeydew and 1/2 cup mango.
- Puree remaining fruit in blender; add orange and lime juice.
- Add tofu and apple juice concentrate; blend.
- Pour into serving bowl. Stir in reserved fruit pieces.

Garnish with fresh strawberries.

Experiment with a variety of melons, and for a change, add ripe bananas. Be creative and use whatever fruits are in season.

SALADS

Wonderful, healthful salads! Crisp, cool salads! Hearty, energy-packed salads!

Salads can enhance a meal, or a salad can be a meal. Enjoy a salad today!

Anytime is a good time for fresh vegetable salads. The key to a good salad is to include a variety of vegetables. The veggies, and sunflower kernels, listed below are some of my favorites for making a great salad.

VEGETABLE SALAD

Spinach	Kale (purple or green)
Leaf lettuce, red	Cauliflower florets
Red bell pepper	Green onions
Mushrooms	Artichoke hearts
Tomatoes	Sunflower kernels, raw

- Wash all vegetables.
- Tear stems from the spinach and kale. Tear leaves into bite size pieces.
- Chop remaining veggies into pieices - all but the tomatoes.
- Add sunflower kernels.
- Add tomatoes just before serving.

DRESSING:

Choose from the vegetable salad dressings beginning on page 57.)

OTHER VEGETABLES
FOR MAKING A GREAT SALAD:

Mustard greens	Broccoli
Romaine lettuce	Squash
Chinese cabbage	Cucumbers
Purple onions	Kohlrabi
Parsley	Watercress
Jicama	Carrots
Cauliflower	Radishes

I'm sure you know of other veggies to use in a salad. The idea is to be creative and use a variety of vegetables each time you make a salad.

Notice that I have not listed head lettuce? As for vitamins, minerals, and fiber, head lettuce is worthless. In order for you to see some of the differences between head and leaf lettuce, I have made a comparison of four vitamins and minerals.

Nutrient	Head Lettuce	Leaf Lettuce	Percent Increase
Beta carotene	9.80 RE*	53.00 RE	540%
Calcium	5.60 mg**	19.00 mg	339%
Iron	0.14 mg	0.39 mg	278%
Potassium	45.00 mg	74.00 mg	164%

* RE = Retinol Equivalents   ** mg = milligrams

Quite impressive! It's easy to see why I recommend leaf lettuce over head lettuce.

By eating nutrient efficient foods, such as the vegetables I have listed, we just naturally build a strong immune system.

In addition to being nutrient-packed, raw vegetables - and fruits - contain live enzymes. Live, active enzymes are vital to good health.

This salad is brimming with nutrients. Notice all the fresh, raw veggies!

Many people like the Mid-East salad called Taboli (Tabbouleh), but the high fat content keeps some people from enjoying it.

The following version is low in fat yet retains all the scrumptious flavor of the high fat version.

TABOLI SALAD

Makes 15, one cup servings

9 cups hot tap water
3 cups (1 pound) taboli wheat (bulgur)*

5 large tomatoes, chopped
2 bunches green onions, chopped
1 bunch fresh parsley, chopped (remove stems)

DRESSING:
1/3 cup sunflower oil**
1/3 cup fresh lemon juice
3 garlic cloves, minced
1 tsp salt

- Put bulgur and water in a bowl. Cover and let set 15 minutes to soften.
- In a very large serving bowl, add chopped vegetables.
- Mix dressing ingredients in a small bowl.
- After bulgur has soaked, drain well; add to veggies.
- Add dressing to mixture. Stir to mix.

If you are sensitive to wheat, use instant brown rice. It works

TABOLI SALAD (Cont'd)

just as well.

This recipe makes a lot of salad, but it keeps quite well in the refrigerator. (It tastes so good it won't last long!)

* Bulgur, or taboli wheat, is cracked wheat that has been partially cooked. In most grocery stores, you will find it in the produce section. To make your own bulgur, see page 113.

** I use cold pressed sunflower oil because it is high in vitamin E. If you want to use another oil, that is fine.

This is a simple yet very tasty salad that Mama used to make. I don't know anyone who doesn't like this salad.

COTTAGE CHEESE VEGETABLE SALAD

Makes 2 1/2 cups

1 cup lowfat cottage cheese*

4 red radishes, thinly sliced

1/2 cup diced cucumber

1/2 cup diced tomato

2 green onions, chopped

Pepper to taste

• Put all ingredients in a serving bowl. Stir to mix.

In this salad we have fresh vegetables which give us a variety of vitamins, minerals, phytochemicals (plant chemicals), and active enzymes. It is important to get fresh, raw fruits and vegetables daily. This is a tasty way to get valuable, active enzymes.

* Choose cottage cheese that is not only low in fat but also does not contain polysorbates and potassium sorbate. To find out more about additives and preservatives in foods, see The Food Storage Bible page 158.

Do you like the bean salads served at salad bars? Those salads are usually very tasty - but they're loaded with fat! Here's a bean salad that's very tasty and has only a small amount of fat.

This dish takes fewer than 10 minutes to throw together! In addition to being quick & tasty, it's nutritious.

RED BEAN SALAD

Makes 5 cups

2 cans (15.5oz each) red beans, drained *(Green Giant)*

1/2 small red onion, cut into rings

1 small green bell pepper, chopped (Use the seeds.)

1 garlic clove, minced

3 TB vinegar

1 TB sunflower oil

2 dashes red pepper sauce *(Tabasco)*

- In a medium salad bowl, combine beans, onion, pepper, and garlic.
- In a small bowl, mix vinegar, oil, and pepper sauce. Add to bean mixture.
- Stir well.

Serve immediately or refrigerate for later.

For a complete meal, add the following:

SERVE WITH THIS:

Whole grain crackers or Guiltless Gourmet Tortilla Chips

Raw veggies such as carrot sticks and cauliflower florets

NOTE: You may certainly use other brands of canned legumes, just be certain there is no EDTA listed as an ingredient. EDTA attracts metals, and we have some very important metals we don't want taken from our bodies; iron, zinc, copper, calcium, etc.

Here is another great bean salad. This is the popular 3-Bean Salad, but without so much fat.

3-BEAN SALAD

Makes 7 cups

1 can (15oz) black beans

1 can (15oz) kidney beans*

1 can (15oz) Great Northern Beans *(Bush's)*

1 bunch green onions, chopped

1 cup chopped cauliflower

1 TB dried parsley or 1/4 cup fresh, chopped

DRESSING:

1 pkt Fat Free Italian Dressing Mix *(Good Seasons)*

1/2 cup water

2 TB vinegar

2 TB apple juice concentrate

1 garlic clove, minced

- Combine beans and vegetables in a large serving bowl.
- Put dressing ingredients in a container with a tight fitting lid.
- Shake well.
- Stir dressing into the bean mixture.

To make a complete protein, just add some whole grain crackers or Guiltless Gourmet Tortilla Chips. (For information about these chips, see page 73.)

* It is difficult to find kidney beans, and some other varieties of canned beans, that do not contain EDTA. Look for brands that are free of this ingredient. EDTA pulls metals from our bodies - metals such as iron, zinc, calcium, and others. For more about chemicals in our foods, and which food products to purchase that are free of harmful chemicals, see *The Food Storage Bible* page 158.

Here is another salad that is a complete meal in itself. It is a complete protein because of the legume (peas) and the grain (corn).

This meal is rounded out with a variety of fresh vegetables; celery, green pepper, and green onions.

This dish is so simple to fix and great to have on hand for busy days.

SOUTHWESTERN SALAD

Makes approximately 5 cups

2 cups frozen peas, thawed

2 cups frozen corn, thawed

1 jar (4oz) chopped pimientos

1 cup chopped celery

1 medium green pepper, chopped (Use the seeds.)

1 bunch green onions, chopped

DRESSING:

1/4 cup vinegar

2 TB water

1 TB cooking oil

1/2 tsp salt

1 garlic clove, minced

Pepper to taste

• Put vegetables in a large serving bowl.
• Mix dressing ingredients in a small bowl.
• Add dressing to vegetables. Stir well.

This dish will keep in the refrigerator for a long time; however, at our house, it is eaten so quickly I don't know for sure how long it will keep!

A handful of Guiltless Gourmet Tortilla Chips is great with this dish. (See page 73.)

This is a fruit salad that can be made any time as these fruits are available throughout the year.

This salad is brimming with live enzymes! Remember, fresh, raw fruits and vegetables contain active enzymes which are essential to good health.

This is a favorite at our house. I hope you like it, too.

MOM'S FRUIT SALAD

Makes approximately 9 cups

3 bananas, sliced

3 oranges, cut in bite size pieces

3 red apples, unpeeled, cut in bite size pieces

1/4 cup orange juice

1/2 cup chopped pecans

- Put ingredients in serving bowl.
- Stir well to mix.

The oranges and orange juice provide citric acid which keeps the bananas and apples from turning dark.

My family likes this salad without a dressing. But if you want a dressing, choose from fruit dressings beginning on page 63.

This is a delightful salad. It has lightness provided by fruit and heartiness provided by brown rice.

FRUIT & BROWN RICE SALAD

Makes 4 servings

1/2 cup instant brown rice*
1/2 cup water

3 medium oranges cut in bite size pieces
1 can (20oz) pineapple chunks, drained
1 cup green grape halves
1/2 cup chopped pecans

- Soak rice in water 30 to 45 minutes.
- Put remaining ingredints in a large serving bowl.
- After rice softens, add to fruit mixture.
- Stir in dressing. (See below.)

DRESSING:
1 cup lowfat cottage cheese**
1 ripe banana
2 TB orange juice

- Put all ingredients in blender; blend until smooth.

This is a very tasty and nutritious salad. Alternate fruits. Use whatever is in season.

* You can use commercial bulgur in place of instant brown rice, or you can make your own. Instructions for making bulgur are on page 113.

** Choose cottage cheese that doesn't contain polysorbates or potassium sorbate.

A fruit salad made with melons is wonderful during the summer when melons are in season. Try a variety of melons with other fruits. Here is a favorite at our house.

MELON FRUIT MEDLEY

Makes about 9 cups

>   3 cups cantaloupe pieces
>
>   2 cups honeydew pieces*
>
>   3 kiwi, peeled and sliced
>
>   2 bananas, sliced
>
>   1 cup sliced strawberries

- Put all ingredients in a large serving bowl. Lightly stir to mix.

This is a fabulous fruit salad! Not only is it beautiful, it tastes scrumptious, and it's packed with nutrients and active enzymes.

If you want a dressing, choose from the fruit dressings beginning on page 63.

* Do you know how to tell when honeydew is ripe? The seeds are loose! Shake a honeydew next to your ear and listen for the seeds to rattle. When you hear seeds, you have a ripe one!

Fresh cabbage is available year round. Since it is packed with nutrients, it's good to have coleslaw frequently. Fix the different versions listed here.

PINEAPPLE COLESLAW

Makes 4 cups

> 3 cups shredded cabbage
>
> 1/2 cup dark raisins
>
> 1 cup drained, crushed pineapple
>
> 2 TB apple juice concentrate
>
> 1/2 cup chopped pecans
>
> 1/2 cup Creamy Yogurt Dressing, page 66.

- Combine all ingredients.

This is a very light, creamy coleslaw - without the fat of traditional coleslaw.

For different tastes, use other fruit dressings beginning on page 63.

This is a different coleslaw because it contains an unusual assortment of vegetables - and cheese. Do give this one a try.

CHEESY GREEN PEA & TOMATO COLESLAW

Makes 5 cups

3 cups shredded cabbage

2 cups frozen peas, thawed

2 medium tomatoes, chopped

1 cup shredded cheddar cheese

CREAMY DRESSING

1 cup firm or extra firm tofu

3 TB apple juice concentrage

- Combine first four ingredients in a serving bowl.
- Put dressing ingredients in blender and blend until smooth.
- Stir dressing into cabbage mixture.

This dish is a complete meal by itself, or it can be served as a side dish.

This is such a simple salad, yet it's so good I serve it to dinner guests.

WHEAT & MUSHROOM SALAD

Serves 6

1 1/2 cups bulgur (taboli wheat)*

6 cups hot tap water

1/4 pound fresh mushrooms, thinly sliced

1 cup chopped green onion

1 /2 cup chopped red bell pepper (Use the seeds.)

VINAIGRETTE DRESSING

1/4 cup rice vinegar**

2 TB cooking oil

1 garlic clove, minced

1 tsp dried oregano

1/4 tsp salt

Pepper to taste

• Put bulgur and water in a bowl. Cover and let set 15 minutes.
• Put remaining vegetables in serving bowl.
• After bulgur has softened, drain well. Add to serving bowl.
• Combine dressing ingredients.
• Add dressing to bulgur mixture. Stir well.

For a complete meal, garnish each serving with thin slices of cheese or slices of hard boiled egg.

Pass the whole grain crackers.

* Bulgur is cracked wheat that has been partially cooked. In most stores, it can be found in the produce section - or you can make your own. Instructions for making bulgur are on page 113.

** Look for rice vinegar that does not contain sulfites.

This is such a pretty salad - as well as a nutritious one.

BROWN RICE
& GARDEN VEGETABLE SALAD

Makes 6 to 8 servings

1 1/2 cups instant brown rice*

1 1/2 cups water

1 medium red bell pepper, chopped (Use the seeds.)

1 medium cucumber, chopped (Do not peel.)**

2 green onions, chopped

1 1/2 cups frozen corn, thawed

Vinaigrette Dressing (See page 61.)

Parsley for garnish

• Soak rice in water 30 to 45 minutes.
• While rice soaks, put vegetables into serving bowl.
• Stir softened rice into veggie mixture.
• Stir in dressing to mix well.
• Garnish with fresh parsley.

Note: For a complete protein, add legumes (beans, peas, or lentils), or some animal food such as cheese, egg, or meat.

* You can use commercial bulgur in place of instant brown rice, or you can make your own. Instructions for making bulgur are on page 113.

** If the cucumber has a tough, bitter skin, peel it; otherwise leave the skin on.

Be creative and use different vegetables - and different cheeses.

This is a most unusual salad, but one that I really enjoy. If you like anchovies, you'll love this salad.

ANCHOVY & LIMA SALAD

Makes 2 to 4 servings

1 can (2oz) anchovy fillets

1 can (16oz) baby lima beans, drained*

DRESSING:

1 tsp finely chopped onion

2 tsp rice vinegar

1 tsp cooking oil

2 TB plain, nonfat yogurt

1 tsp dried parsley flakes

Lettuce leaves

Tomato wedges

- Drain oil from anchovy fillets.
- Press paper towels into fillets to remove excess oil.
- Chop fillets into *very* small pieces. Put in serving bowl.
- Add drained lima beans.
- Put dressing ingredients in small bowl; stir.
- Stir dressing into bean mixture.

Serve on lettuce leaves with tomato wedges as garnish. Pass the whole grain crackers.

* Choose baby lima beans without EDTA

This is such a simple salad. Quick to fix, tasty, nutritious, and pretty.

TANGY TOMATOES

Makes 8 servings

2 cups drained, lowfat cottage cheese*

1/2 cup chopped cucumbers

1/2 cup chopped celery

1/2 cup chopped green onion

1 grapefruit, peeled and diced

Pepper to taste

8 medium tomatoes

8 lettuce leaves

- Combine first 6 ingredients. Mix well.
- Put lettuce leaves on serving plates.
- Cut tomatoes into fourths; arrange on lettuce leaves.
- Spoon cottage cheese mixture into center of each tomato.

Pass the whole grain crackers.

This is a taste treat with the combination of vegetables and grapefruit. Unusual, but very good.

* Choose cottage cheese without polysorbates or potassium sorbate.

What a pretty salad this is with the brightly colored bell peppers. This salad is simple and tasty.

BELL PEPPER SALAD

Makes 4 servings

　　　1 medium red bell pepper

　　　1 medium yellow bell pepper

　　　1 medium green bell pepper

　　　1/2 cup sliced black olives

　　　2 TB capers

　　　1 TB rice vinegar*

　　　2 tsp cooking oil

- Cut peppers into 1/4 inch strips.
- Put into a 9 x 13 baking dish.
- Combine remaining ingredients in a small bowl.
- Add to pepper strips. Mix well.
- Cover and refrigerate - or eat right away. (Flavors will mix when mixture sets for a few hours.)

NOTE: If you're not familiar with capers, look for them near the olives. I think you'll like the flavor capers give to dishes. FYI: Capers are wonderful as a topper for deviled eggs.

* Look for rice vinegar that does not contain sulfites.

This is a wonderful salad. Great flavor!

LEBANESE SALAD

Makes 4 servings

> 1 cup instant brown rice*
>
> 1 cup water
>
> 20 dried apricot halves, chopped**
>
> 10 dates, chopped
>
> 1/4 cup chopped fresh parsley (or 1 TB dried)
>
> 1 TB cooking oil
>
> 2 TB orange juice

- Soak rice in water 30 to 45 minutes.
- In serving bowl, combine remaining ingredients.
- After rice has softened, add to serving bowl. Stir well to mix.

This salad has a slightly sweet flavor. Very unusual - and *very* good!

---

* You can use commercial bulgur in place of instant brown rice, or you can make your own. Instructions for making bulgur are on page 113.

** Purchase unsulfured apricots. You will find these in some grocery stores and health food stores. Many light colored, dried fruits have been sulfured. Look for the ingredient 'sulfur dioxide'. Many people, particularly those with allergies and/or asthma are sensitive to sulfites. To learn more about harmful additives and preservatives, see *The Food Storage Bible* page 158.

This is a delightfully light, summer salad.

CREAMY CUCUMBER SALAD

Makes 4 servings

2 large cucumbers

1 cup lowfat cottage cheese

2 tsp dried dill weed*

1 small garlic clove, minced

- Score and thinly slice cucumbers.**
- Put cucumbers in serving dish.
- Put remaining ingredients in blender; blend until smooth.
- Add cottage cheese mixture to cucumbers. Stir well.

The flavors will blend if this salad is covered and refrigerated for a couple hours. If you're in a hurry, go ahead and eat it immediately.

* If you have fresh dill, by all means use it.

** To score cucumbers, run fork tines down length of cucumber, making parallel lines in peel.

Serve this salad to your anchovy lovers. It will be a hit!

This is a great summer salad. If you have your own garden tomatoes or can purchase locally grown tomatoes, this salad will have even better flavor.

TOMATO - MUSHROOM SALAD

Makes 4 servings

3 medium tomatoes, coarsley chopped

6 medium, fresh mushrooms, thinly sliced

2 TB chopped, fresh parsley

2 TB fresh lemon juice

2 TB cooking oil

1/4 tsp salt

Pepper to taste

Lettuce leaves

- Combine tomatoes, mushrooms, and parsley in mixing bowl.
- In a container with tight fitting lid, combine lemon juice, oil, salt and pepper. Shake to mix.
- Pour dressing over tomato mixture. Stir well.
- Serve on lettuce leaves.

For better flavor, cover this dish and let set in the refrigerator a couple hours.

Beets are a very nutritious food. But for some reason, we usually don't eat many beets. Give this salad a try. You may eat beets more often!

BEET SALAD

Makes 4 servings

1 can (15oz) beets, sliced

1 small white onion, thinly sliced

DRESSING:

1/2 cup fat free sour cream *(Daisy)*

1 tsp fresh lemon juice

1/8 tsp salt

Pepper to taste

4 lettuce leaves

- On each lettuce leaf, arrange beet and onion slices.
- In a small bowl, combine dressing ingredients.
- Top each serving with dressing.

This is a *very* quick and easy salad. Do give this one a try.

This is a familiar salad, but without all the fat of the original salad.

CARROT - RAISIN - PINEAPPLE SALAD

Makes 4 cups

> 3 cups grated carrots (about 5 medium carrots)
>
> 3/4 cup dark raisins
>
> 1/2 cup drained, crushed pineapple
>
> 2 TB apple juice concentrate
>
> 3/4 cup Creamy Yogurt Dressing, page 66

• Combine all ingredients in serving bowl. Stir well.

This is a light, creamy version of Carrot - Raisin Salad - not the

This is a hearty, stick-to-the-ribs salad.

BUTTER BEAN SALAD

Makes 5 cups

1 can (16oz) large butter beans, undrained *(Bush's)**

1 large tomato, chopped

1/2 cup chopped green onion

1 TB vinegar

1 tsp dried parsley

1 tsp dried oregano

Feta cheese**

- In a serving bowl, combine ingredients through oregano.
- Top lightly with crumbled feta cheese.

Pass the whole grain crackers.

---

* Purchase any brand of butter bean that does not contain EDTA. Look at the ingredient label to find EDTA.

** Use the cheese you like. But use only a small amount as cheese is high in fat.

MEDITERRANIAN DELIGHT

Makes 8 to 10 servings

1 1/2 cups dry garbanzo beans*

1 large unpeeled cucumber, chopped**
2 medium tomatoes, chopped
1 small red onion, chopped
1/2 cup fresh, chopped parsley
3/4 cup black olive halves

DRESSING
1/4 cup fresh lemon juice
1/4 cup cooking oil
2 cloves garlic, minced
1/2 tsp salt

Feta cheese

- Soak garbanzo beans in 3 cups water overnight.
- To fix salad, drain beans. Put in large serving bowl.
- Add cucumber, tomato, onion, parsley, and olives.
- In small bowl, prepare dressing.
- Add dressing to vegetable mixture. Stir well.

Top each serving with a small amount of crumbled feta cheese.
Pass the crackers. Whole grain, of course!

---

* Garbanzo beans soaked overnight will be a bit crunchy - not soft. If you want soft beans, cook the soaked garbanzos for about 30 minutes - or purchase canned garbanzos. Just be certain canned beans do not contain EDTA.

** If the cucumber has a tough, bitter skin, peel it.

typical high fat variety.

Stuffed tomatoes make a festive looking salad. This one not only looks good, it tastes good!

DILLY STUFFED TOMATOES

Makes 2 servings

2 large tomatoes

1/2 cup Tofu Mayonnaise Spread*
1/2 tsp dried dill weed

2 lettuce leaves

- Cut tops from tomatoes.
- Scoop out pulp, leaving enough around edges to hold filling.
- Chop tomato pulp and put in mixing bowl.
- Add Tofu Mayonnaise Spread and dill weed. Mix well.
- Stuff tomato shells. Arrange on lettuce leaves.

The next time you want to fix something special, give this dish a try!

* For Tofu Mayonnaise Spread, see page 80.

DRESSINGS

A great salad deserves a great dressing - one that doesn't overpower it. Turn the page for some scrumptious vegetable and fruit salad dressings.

Many people want a fat free salad dressing. This is evident by the number of fat free dressings available on our grocery shelves! Most of these dressings are quite high in sugar and contain harmful additives and preservatives.

If you like the mustard flavor, you will like this dressing for a vegetable salad.

GERMAN MUSTARD DRESSING

Makes 1 cup

1 cup water

3 TB German mustard

1 small garlic clove, minced

2 tsp dried basil

- Put all ingredients in a glass jar with a tight fitting lid.
- Shake until well mixed.

Use right away or refrigerate for later use.

Because this salad dressing does not contain oil, it is 'runny'. That's okay, but just be aware that it won't stick to the veggies like an oil-based dressing.

If you like 3-Bean Salad, you'll love this dressing. The dressing on most 3-Bean Salads is *very* high in fat and sugar, but not this one.

This dressing is great on a variety of salads, not just a bean salad. Give it a try. I think you'll like the flavor.

3-BEAN SALAD DRESSING

Makes 3/4 cup

1 pkt Fat Free Italian Dressing Mix *(Good Seasons)**

1/2 cup water

2 TB vinegar

2 TB apple juice concentrate

1 garlic clove, minced

- Put ingredients in a container with tight fitting lid. Shake until well mixed.

This dressing is great on vegetable salads, particularly those that contain legumes (beans) as well as sprouts.

* Many brands of salad dressings and salad dressing mixes contain harmful additives or preservatives. This particular dressing mix by Good Seasons is free of these harmful ingredients.

Many people like to use herb vinegars when making salad dressings. Herbed vinegars are so tasty - and attractive. What is so eye-catching about these vinegars are the **fresh** herbs floating in a pretty bottle.

When making herbed vinegars, you can use a variety of herbs as well as a variety of vinegars.

Here are some of my favorite fresh herb choices:

> Tarragon   Basil
>
> Oregano   Dill

Below are some of the vinegars I like to use:

> Natural Rice Vinegar
>
> Apple Cider Vinegar
>
> Distilled White Vinegar
>
> Seasoned Rice Vinegar

There are some popular vinegars on the market that I will not use because they contain sulfites. Look at the ingredient label to identify those with sulfites

HERB VINEGAR

Crush a sprig of 1 or 2 fresh herbs between your fingers and add to 1 cup vinegar of choice. Add I or 2 garlic cloves cut in half. Put in a sunny window for a few hours for flavors to mix.

To make vinegar & oil dressing:

To 1/2 cup herb vinegar, add 2 TB oil.

Most vinegar and oil salad dressings contain *much* more oil. In fact, it's usually 1 cup oil to 1/2 cup vinegar.

NOTE: I use cold pressed sunflower oil because it has more vitamin E than most oils.

Vinaigrette dressings are some of my favorites. I love the flavor that various of herbs lend to this dressing.

HERB DIJON VINAIGRETTE DRESSING

Makes about 1 cup

    1/4 cup water

    1/4 cup rice vinegar*

    1 envelope *Lipton Savory Herb with Garlic*

    1/2 tsp dried oregano**

    1/2 tsp dried parsley

    1/2 tsp dried basil

    1 medium garlic clove, minced

    2 TB Dijon mustard

    2 TB cooking oil

    Pepper to taste

• Combine all ingredients in a pretty bottle or cruet.

Serve with vegetable salads.

* Choose a rice vinegar that does not contain sulfites.
** If you have fresh herbs, by all means use them instead of the dried herbs.

If you like a creamy ranch-type dressing, but don't want the fat, sugar or preservatives in most ranch dressings, serve this one.

CREAMY RANCH DRESSING

Makes about 1 cup

1 cup low fat cottage cheese*
1 TB salad seasoning**
1 small garlic clove, minced

• Put all ingredients in blender; blend until smooth.

Serve with vegetable salads.

NOTE: If you prefer a thinner dressing, just add skim milk.

* Choose a cottage cheese that does not contain polysorbates or potassium sorbate.

** Use a variety of seasonings to make different flavored dressings.
These are spices I use:

Basil	Dill
Celery seed	Horseradish, prepared
Cilantro	Oregano
Curry	

Be creative, and experiment with different flavors.

Fruit salads are wonderful. If you like a creamy dressing but don't want the fat that a creamy dressing usually contains, you'll want to fix this one.

SOUR CREAM FRUIT DRESSING

Makes 1/2 cup

1/2 cup fat free sour cream*

1 TB apple juice concentrate

1 TB orange juice

• Put all ingredients in a small bowl. Mix well.

Serve over your favorite fruit salad.

Regular sour cream is *very* high in fat . Notice the difference between these two kinds of sour cream. A serving is 2 tablespoons.

	Regular Sour Cream	Fat Free Sour Cream
Calories	60	20
Fat	5 g	0
% Calories from fat	75%	0

* Choose a fat free sour cream that does not contain potassium sorbate or artificial colors.

I like to include tofu in my diet each day - but it has to taste good. If I can taste the tofu, it isn't good! I hope you give my tofu recipes a try, but if you have folks who turn up their noses at the word 'tofu', don't tell them.

TOFU FRUIT DRESSING

Makes 1 cup

> 1 cup firm or extra firm tofu
>
> 1 ripe banana
>
> 2 TB orange juice

- Put all ingredients in blender; blend until smooth.

Serve over fruit.

This is so simple and so very tasty. Give it a try.

Do you remember when people used to turn up their noses at the word 'yogurt' - just like they do tofu now? Yogurt has finally been accepted. (Maybe tofu will be eventually. I hope so!)

This is a very tasty dressing using yogurt.

ORANGE YOGURT DRESSING

Makes 2/3 cup

1/3 cup plain, nonfat yogurt

1/3 cup orange juice

1 TB apple juice concentrate

• Put ingredients in blender; blend until smooth.

Serve this light, creamy dressing over fruit.

This is another yogurt dressing that has a very fresh flavor.

CREAMY YOGURT DRESSING

Makes 1 cup

1 cup plain, nonfat yogurt

1 TB fresh lemon juice

2 TB apple juice concentrate

1/4 tsp salt

• Put ingredients in blender; blend until smooth.

This dressing is very light, and is great with fruit salad.

I like this dressing served over sliced bananas and strawberries. It's also good over sliced bananas and chopped prunes.

I call this "Best Fruit Dressing" because it is by far the best fruit dressing I've ever tasted - and I've tasted a few!

This dressing is very creamy yet has very little fat.

BEST FRUIT DRESSING

Makes about 1 1/4 cups

      1 cup low fat cottage cheese

      1 ripe banana

      2 TB orange juice

- Put ingredients in blender; blend until smooth.

Serve over any mixture of fruit.

I hope you like this one. As I said, this is my favorite.

You can make a variety of scrumptious creamy dressings using cottage cheese. Here are a few:

CREAMY PINEAPPLE - BANANA DRESSING

Makes 1 1/4 cups

> 1 cup lowfat cottage cheese
>
> 1 ripe banana
>
> 1/4 cup crushed pineapple*

• Put ingredients in blender; blend until smooth.

Serve over fruit salad containing pineapple.

Examples:

Pineapple/banana

Pineapple/Banana/Mango

Pineapple/Banana/Grape

* Use canned pineapple that does not contain sugar.

If you want a change from the flavor of banana, use only pineapple:

CREAMY PINEAPPLE DRESSING

Makes 1 cup

1 cup lowfat cottage cheese

1/2 cup crushed pineapple

• Put ingredients in blender; blend until smooth.

Again, use this dressing over fruit that contains pineapple.

* * *

More variations to "Best Fruit Dressing".....

These two dressings are great for fruit salads that contain apples.

CREAMY APPLE - BANANA DRESSING

Makes 1 cup

1 cup lowfat cottage cheese

1 ripe banana

1/4 cup apple juice concentrate

• Put ingredients in blender; blend until smooth.

This dressing is wonderful for Waldorf Salad - or any salad that contains apples.

If you want just a creamy apple dressing, try this one:

CREAMY APPLE DRESSING

Makes 3/4 cup

1 cup lowfat cottage cheese

1/4 cup apple juice concentrate

• Put ingredients in blender; blend until smooth.

Use on any fruit salad that contains apples.

* * *

Here is another wonderful creamy dressing. Please choose only white grape juice that I recommend.

CREAMY GRAPE DRESSING

Makes 3/4 cup

1 cup lowfat cottage cheese

1/4 cup white grape juice*

• Put ingredients in blender; blend until smooth.

This is wonderful on any fruit salad containing grapes.

* NOTE: Use only white grape juice that does not contain sulfites. Very few brands of white grape juice are free of sulfites. In most grocery stores, you can avoid sulfites by purchasing white grape juice in the baby food section.

People with allergies and/or asthma are most susceptible to sulfites. In some people, the throat may swell, thus closing the windpipe. For more information about harmful additives and preservatives in foods, see *The Food Storage Bible*, page 158.

SANDWICHES

Whoever invented the sandwich did us a great service!

A sandwich can be something very nutritious - or it can be a health hazzard. We're going to look only at those that are healthful, as well as tasty.

Most men really like sandwiches. They also like them to be simple. So up front, we'll look at the best choices when it comes to sandwich fixins' using luncheon meats and the trimmings.

BREAD...

The first thing a sandwich needs is something to hold it together - bread. The best bread is a whole grain bread. There are wonderful choices in health food stores. Try the different varieties offered there.

In the 'regular' grocery store, our choices are greatly limited when it comes to whole grain. You will find a *few* loaves of Whole Wheat Bread. Notice the word 'whole'. This is a significant word. To be whole wheat bread, the first ingredient listed must be 'whole wheat flour'.

The next best choice is Wheat Berry Bread. The first ingredient is enriched flour which is *not* whole wheat, but the second ingredient is 'cracked wheat berries', and the third ingredient is 'whole wheat flour'.

LUNCHEON MEATS OR DELI MEATS...

Are we ever limited when it comes to meats! Most meats; beef, pork, chicken, and turkey, contain sodium nitrite. What's so bad about nitrites? Nitrites combine with stomach juices to form powerful cancer-causing agents called nitrosamines.

So what meats do not contain nitrites? Very few! Here is a list:

Sliced Turkey:	Louis Rich Oven Roasted Turkey Breast
Sliced Turkey:	Oscar Mayer Oven Roasted White Turkey
Sliced Chicken:	Louis Rich Carving Board Grilled Chicken Breast
Chunk Turkey:	Louis Rich Oven Roasted Breast of Turkey
Chunk Turkey:	Butterball Breast of Turkey
In the deli:	
Sliced Turkey:	Deli Perfect Gourmet, Cajun Style Breast of Turkey
Sliced Beef:	Kentuckian Gold Beef Roast

Notice there is no ham, turkey ham, bologna, pastrami, etc? These all contain nitrities. When you look at labels on cured meats, look for sodium nitrite or nitrate. If you see either one, leave it on the shelf!

VEGETABLES...

Lettuce: Use only leaf lettuce or other leafy greens such as spinach, kale, etc. Head lettuce is practically void of vitamins, minerals, and fiber.

Tomatoes: Tomatoes are great on sandwiches. Choose those that are produced in the United States. Why? Produce raised in other countries can have pesticides that are banned in the U.S..

Onions: Onions add zing to any sandwich. And onions are *very* healthful. Any onion is good. The hotter the onion, the more health benefits it has.

SPREADS...

Some people like mustard others like mayonnaise. Most mustards are free of harmful additives or preservatives. Not so for mayo. It is difficult to find a mayonnaise that doesn't contain EDTA. A good choice of mayo is made by Hain. It can be found in some grocery stores and in most health food stores. Another good mayo-type spread is Nayonaise. This spread is made from soybeans and is quite tasty. Look for this one in large grocery stores or health food stores.

CHEESE...

Some people like to add cheese to a sandwich. If you add cheese, the best choice is an unprocessed cheese. (Many processed cheeses contain aluminum.) Choose a natural cheese such as mozzarella, Swiss, cheddar, etc. It is best to use only a small amount of cheese as it is high in saturated fat.

CHIPS...

If you're a chip eater, there are some good choices, particularly when it comes to tortilla chips. The best tortilla chip I've ever eaten is made by Guiltless Gourmet*. The following varieties are available in a 7 ounce bag ; Yellow Corn, Yellow Corn - Unsalted, Sweet White Corn, Organic Blue Corn, Organic Red Corn, Spicy Black Bean, Picante Ranch, Chili Lime, and Mucho Nacho. (Guiltless Gourmet has most of these varieties available in the 1 ounce, snack-size bag.)

*HOT TIP. If you can't find Guiltless Gourmet Chips, call the company; 1-800-723-9541.

Another choice is Regular, Low Fat Baked Tostitos. The taste and texture isn't nearly as good as Guiltless Gourmet, but there are no harmful additives or preservatives - and it is low in fat.

As for potato chips, most are very high in fat. The best choice I could find was Ruffles, Reduced Fat Potato Chips. Below is a comparison between Ruffles Reduced Fat and Ruffles Regular Potato Chips.

RUFFLES POTATO CHIPS	SERVING	CALORIES	FAT	% FAT
Ruffles, Reduced Fat	16 chips	140	60 calories	43%
Ruffles, Regular	12 chips	160	90 calories	56%

SPROUTS...

If you haven't eaten sprouts on a sandwich, you've missed something! Sprouting is very simple and can add abundant nutrients to a sandwich. For simple sprouting directions, see page 145.

Some of the best seeds to sprout for sandwiches are:

Alfalfa	Clover	Radish
Buckwheat	Lentils	Quinoa

Give these a try. I think you'll like them.

FINGER VEGGIES...

To make a great meal using a sandwich as the main course, just add healthful corn chips and raw veggies. There are many choices of raw veggies. Choose a variety such as the ones below from your produce section:

Carrot	Cauliflower	Broccoli
Celery	Radish	Bell pepper
Cucumber	Summer squash	Turnip
Sweet potato	Jicama	

A sandwich with these trimmings makes for a very nutritious meal. I nearly always have ingredients on hand for this quick, tasty, and healthful meal.

If you serve sandwiches at your house, fix them with these ingredients, and you'll feel good about serving a 'Sandwich Dinner.'

* * *

We can't forget the all-time favorite - the Peanut Butter Sandwich. But have you ever tried a Soy Butter Sandwich? The 'butter' is made from the same legume family, but the legume is soybeans instead of peanuts.

You can find soy butter in larger grocery stores or in health food stores. Soy butter is a tasty way to get important plant estrogen.

PEANUT BUTTER SANDWICHES...

There are some excellent brands of peanut butter on our shelves - and some not so good. One of the best brands is Arrowhead Mills. The only ingredient is 100% peanuts. There are other excellent brands. Use *The Food Storage Bible* to help choose other quality brands. (See page 158.)

Just so you will know what some of the highly advertised brands contain, read on:

BRAND	INGREDIENT
Jif	Sugar and oil added
Reese's	Sugar and cottonseed oil*
Peter Pan	Sugar and cottonseed oil

*Cotton is not a food crop, and chemicals banned for use on food crops do not apply to cotton.

BREAD...

Again, the best bread is a whole grain bread. Look for "Whole" Wheat Bread or Wheat Berry Bread.

FRUIT...

If you haven't tried fresh fruit mixed into peanut or soy butter, you've missed something! My children and grandchildren love a mashed, ripe banana mixed in their peanut butter. There are other fresh fruits they like; peaches, apricots and any kind of berry.

Note: Fruits must be ripe or over-ripe to have the sweet flavor that goes so well with peanut or soy butter.

JAMS...

There are some wonderful jams on the market that are made with only fruit and fruit juices. (No refined sugar here!) Two that are on my grocer's shelves are Smucker's Simply Fruit and Polaner Jams.

One of my favorite 'butter' sandwiches, is peanut or soy butter mixed with apple butter. I just love this! The apple butter I use is Reese Apple Butter Spread. It is made with apples and apple cider. That's all. No refined sugar.

A peanut or soy butter sandwich is quite healthful - and also quite high in fat. Because of the fat, we don't want to go overboard.

When we have a peanut butter/banana sandwich on whole grain bread - with raw veggies on the side, we have a nutritious meal. Enjoy - just not too often!

Many people enjoy tuna salad sandwiches. The drawback to this great sandwich spread is the fat. Most all 'spreads' are high in fat because of the mayonnaise. Well, in this spread, there is no mayonnaise. Because of no mayo, this spread will not be as creamy or rich as the high fat varieties.

TUNA SALAD SANDWICH SPREAD

Makes 1 cup

> 1 can (6.5oz) water pack tuna, drained*
>
> 1/4 cup finely chopped celery
>
> 1/4 cup chopped green onion
>
> 1 TB dried parsley**
>
> 1/3 cup plain, nonfat yogurt
>
> 1 tsp fresh lemon juice
>
> 1 TB prepared, spicy mustard

- Mix all ingredients thoroughly.
- Spread on whole grain bread or…
- Use as a filling in whole wheat pita pockets.

How simple can you get!! I nearly always have ingredients on hand to throw this spread together when I need a really quick meal.

Just add some raw veggies on the side, as well as some Guiltless Gourmet chips, and you have a great meal in a very few minutes.

* You can certainly use other canned seafood as well as chicken or turkey.

** If you have fresh parsley, by all means use it. Fresh is always best.

Do you like pizza? Who doesn't! Why not have a pizza sandwich? This is so simple and soooo tasty.

PIZZA SANDWICH

Makes 1 sandwich

> 2 slices whole grain bread
>
> 2 thin slices low moisture, part skim mozzarella cheese*
>
> Pizza or spaghetti sauce

- Put 1 slice cheese on 1 slice of bread.
- Spread sauce over cheese.
- Top with remaining cheese and bread.

Kids love this sandwich - and it's simple enough to make that most children can fix their own.

EAT WITH THIS:

A variety of fresh veggies such as:

Carrot sticks, cauliflower florets, cucumber slices, etc.

---

* Have you ever eaten soy mozzarella cheese? It's great. For a change, give it a try.

When packing lunches, do you sometimes want a good sandwich that won't spoil easily? Peanut butter is always a good choice; but, as we know, peanut butter is very high in fat. So, what's another good choice? How about using another legume besides peanuts? How about Great Northern Beans or black beans?

This is a bean spread that is tasty - and so simple to make. Your children will love helping you fix it. (Remember, children are much more likely to eat what they've helped prepare.)

HERBED BEAN SPREAD

Makes 1 cup

      1 can (16oz) Great Northern Beans, *(Bush's)*

      1 TB fresh lemon juice

      1 garlic clove, minced

      1 tsp capers*

      1/2 tsp cooking oil

      1 1/2 tsp dried Italian spices

      1/4 tsp pepper

- Drain & rinse beans. Put in blender or food processor and blend until smooth. (Or put beans on a plate, and mash with a fork.)
- Add remaining ingredients. Mix well.

Serve on whole wheat bread or wrap in whole wheat tortillas.

Add fresh spinach or leaf lettuce, a slice of tomato and onion.

SERVE WITH THIS:

A variety of raw veggies.

---

* Capers add a delightful touch to this spread. You will find capers near the olives.

Have you been looking for a substitute for mayonnaise that is tasty, nutritious and low in fat? Well here is a great sandwich spread! This one is made with tofu.

I don't know about you, but tofu just doesn't turn me on. Tofu has to be well camouflaged for me to like it. Well, let me tell you, this stuff is good!

I spread this on a whole grain cracker, whole grain bagel, or whole grain bread. It's wonderful!

TOFU SPREAD & MAYONNAISE

Makes approximately 2 cups

1 pkg (12.3oz) *Mori-Nu Lite Tofu*, firm or extra firm

1 1/2 TB fresh lemon juice

1 1/2 TB cooking oil

1/2 tsp. salt

• Mix ingredients in a blender or food processor. Refrigerate and use as needed.

It's quite simple to make a light meal using this mixture. Just spread it on whole grain crackers or whole grain bread; add sliced tomato, spinach leaves, onion, etc. - and raw veggies on the side. Presto, a quick lunch.

(The soybeans of the tofu, and the whole grain in the crackers or bread make this a complete protein.)

There are times when we want to serve open-faced sandwiches. Maybe for a bridal shower, a luncheon - or you just want to fix something special for your family. Open-faced, finger sandwiches can provide that special touch.

OPEN-FACED DILLY SANDWICH

Makes 1/2 cup

1/2 cup Tofu Mayonnaise Spread*
1/2 tsp dried dill weed

Whole grain bread or whole grain crackers

1 cucumber, scored and thinly sliced**

- Mix spread and dill weed.
- Spread on whole grain bread or crackers.
- Top with cucumber slices.

This makes a marvelous open-faced, finger sandwich. For a nice effect, you may want to first toast your bread, trim off the crust, and cut into fourths before adding the spread.

Be creative, and try a variety of spices or fresh herbs. Remember that flavors will become more robust after they've had a chance to set for a while.

* For Tofu Mayonnaise Spread, see page 80.

** To score cucumber, run fork tines down length of cucumber, making parallel lines in the skin.

This is another very tasty dilly sandwich spread, but this one is made with fat free sour cream instead of tofu. (My family prefers the taste of the dilly spread made with tofu. Go figure when not one of us likes the taste of plain tofu!) Fix both recipes, and you decide which you like best.

SOUR CREAM & DILL SANDWICH SPREAD

Makes 1/2 cup

1/2 cup fat free sour cream

1/2 tsp dried dill weed

1/4 tsp salt

1 cucumber, scored*

Whole grain bread or whole grain crackers

- Mix sour cream, dill, and salt.
- Spread on whole grain bread or crackers.
- Top with cucumber slices

This makes a marvelous open-faced, finger sandwich. For a nice effect, toast your bread, trim the crust, and cut into fourths before adding the spread.

* To score cucumber, run fork tines down length of cucumber, making parallel lines in the skin.

Want a dilly sandwich with a twist? This one has a robust flavor with the addition of horseradish. I like the 'bite' horseradish gives.

DILLY - HORSERADISH SANDWICH SPREAD

Makes 1/2 cup

1/2 cup fat free cream cheese, softened

2 TB plain, nonfat yogurt

2 tsp prepared horseradish*

1/2 tsp dried dill weed

1 cucumber, scored and sliced

- Place ingredients, all but cucumber slices, on a plate.
- Mash with a fork to mix well.
- Spread on whole grain bread.
- Top with cucumber slices.

This is a great spread on whole grain bread or a whole grain bagel. If you like a hotter spread, use more horseradish.

* Prepared horseradish is found in the refrigerated section of your grocery store.

This is another special sandwich spread that makes a good party sandwich. The flavor is unique - but great.

OLIVE - NUT SPREAD

Makes about 1 cup

1 pkg (3oz) low fat cream cheese, softened

1/2 cup finely chopped English walnuts

1/4 cup chopped pimento-stuffed, green olives*

2 TB milk or soy milk

- Stir all ingredients until well mixed.
- Cut whole wheat bread slices into four pieces. (Trim crust if you'd like.)
- Spread mixture onto bread slices. Top with second slice of bread.

This spread makes wonderful small sandwiches for any party - or a special treat for your family.

* Choose green olives that do not contain sodium alginate or potassium sorbate.

Another great sandwich spread that's very tasty, easy to fix and nutritious is shrimp salad spread. Most shrimp spreads are high in fat - but not this one.

SHRIMP SALAD SANDWICH

Makes about 1 cup

1 can (4.5oz) broken shrimp, drained

2 TB finely chopped celery

1 TB fresh lemon juice

3 TB Tofu Mayonnaise*

1/8 tsp salt

Pepper to taste

• Stir together all ingredients until well mixed.

This makes a great sandwich - whether it's a finger sandwich for a fancy party, or it's a 'regular' sandwich for hungry family members.

For party sandwiches, trim crust from whole grain bread, and cut into shapes; triangles, squares, etc. Serve party sandwiches open-faced. (No bread on top.)

* For Tofu Mayonnaise Spread, see page 80.

This is a delightful sandwich spread. It's not only tasty, it's very nutritious.

SEAFOOD SANDWICH SPREAD

Makes 3 cups

2 cups firm or extra firm tofu

1 envelope *Lipton Onion Soup Mix*

2 tsp fresh lemon juice

2 TB liquid from canned salmon

1 cup drained, canned salmon*

2 green onions chopped

1/2 cup chopped celery

- In blender or food processor, blend until smooth; tofu, soup mix, lemon juice and salmon liquid.
- Put mixture in bowl; stir in salmon, green onions, and celery.

Spread this mixture on whole grain bread. Add fresh spinach or leaf lettuce and a tomato slice.

* For variety, use canned tuna or mackerel.

MAIN DISHES

I have always liked one-dish main meals. They're quick - and only one serving dish to wash!

The meals in this section are very simple, and at the same time, they're very nutritious. You can feel good about serving these to your family.

This dish is soooo easy to fix, and most everyone loves it. Do give this one a try.

QUICK MEXICAN SALAD

Makes 6 servings

1 can (15oz each)

> Black beans
>
> Chili Hot Beans *(Bush's)*
>
> Great Northern Beans *(Bush's)*
>
> (Drain all beans, but do not rinse.)

1 large red bell pepper, chopped (Use the seeds.)*

2/3 cup mild salsa *(Pace)*

1/2 cup chopped green onions

1 garlic clove, minced

4 oz shredded, low moisture, part skim mozzarella cheese

- Put all ingredients in a serving bowl - all but the cheese. Stir well.
- Serve the mozzarella on the side, and top each serving with a *small* amount of cheese.

This is fantastic served with cornbread. If you don't want to make cornbread, pass the Guiltless Gourmet Tortilla Chips. (See page 73.)

---

* Notice that anytime I use bell peppers I say, "Use the seeds". Most all recipes tell us to discard the seeds. Have you ever wondered why we're told to throw away these seeds? Think about it, wheat is a seed, rice is a seed, the beans in this dish are seeds. Seeds are *very* nutritious. They are the life of a food. Eat those seeds!

Here is a popular Mexican dish that's a favorite at our house.

Do you know what Arroz con Pollo means? 'Arroz' is rice, 'con' is with, and 'pollo' is chicken. This is Rice With Chicken. Do give it a try.

ARROZ CON POLLO

Makes 6 servings

2 cups instant brown rice*

2 cups hot tap water

1 can (10oz) white chicken, drained *(Swanson)*

1/2 tsp cumin

1/2 tsp chili powder

1 small onion, chopped

1 garlic clove, minced

1 can (14.5oz) stewed tomatoes

1/3 cup picante sauce *(Pace)*

1 can (8oz) kidney beans, drained *(S&W)*

- Soak rice in water 30 to 45 minutes.
- While rice soaks, put remaining ingredients in a large serving dish.
- Add softened rice to chicken mixture. Stir well.

To finish off this meal, I would add a fresh vegetable salad. What a great meal you have now!

---

* In place of instant brown rice, you can use bulgur. You can purchase bulgur, or you can make your own. Instructions for making bulgur are on page 113.

How about a really quick Mexican dish that tastes sooooo good? You can have this dish on the table in 10 minutes - or less, if you're really fast.

This dish is packed with energy, and it's very low in fat.

LAYERED FIESTA DINNER

Makes 4 large servings

2 cans (16oz each) black refried beans *(Rosarita)*

1 cup fat free sour cream*

1/2 cup picante sauce *(Pace)*

1 large tomato, chopped

1 bunch green onions, chopped

1 can (2.25oz) sliced ripe olives, drained

Sour cream for garnish

- In a serving dish, layer each ingredient in the order given. (Use a clear serving dish if possible.)
- Top off this meal with a dollop of sour cream. (A dollop is a hefty spoon full.)

Pass the Guiltless Gourmet Tortilla Chips. (See page 73.)

SERVE WITH THIS:

Raw veggies such as carrot sticks, cauliflower florets, slices of bell pepper, etc. - whatever your family enjoys.

---

* Choose a fat free sour cream that does not contain potassium sorbate, artificial color or artificial flavor.

I recently had this wonderful dish in Santa Fe, New Mexico. It was served as a side dish, but I could have eaten more of this and forgotten the rest of the meal.

This is a complete meal in itself. (The peas and corn make a complete protein.) This dish is loaded with energy, it's extremely low in fat and can be tossed together in minutes. What a deal!

SANTA FE DELIGHT

Makes 4 cups

1 cup frozen peas, thawed

1 cup frozen corn, thawed

1 red bell pepper, chopped (Use the seeds.)

1 green bell pepper, chopped (Use the seeds.)

1/2 cup chopped green onions

2/3 cup chopped, fresh cilantro leaves*

DRESSING:

1/2 cup water

2 TB vinegar

4 tsp cooking oil

1/2 tsp salt

1 garlic clove, minced

• Put first group of ingredients in a serving dish.

• Mix dressing ingredients in small bowl.

• Add dressing to vegetable mixture. Stir well.

Pass the Guiltless Gourmet Tortilla Chips. (See page 73.)

* The fresh cilantro just 'makes' this dish. It would not be the same without it. Cilantro is one of the herbs that gives Mexican food its unique flavor. If you are not familiar with it, you will find it in the produce section near the parsley.

Mexican flavored dishes are very popular. This dish has a special Southwest flavor. It's one of our favorites. See what you think.

ALBUQUERQUE SPECIAL

Makes 4 large servings

2 cups instant brown rice*
1 can (14.5oz) chicken broth *(Swanson 1/3 Less Sodium)*

1 garlic clove, minced
1 small onion, chopped
2 small zucchini, thinly sliced
2 cans (14.5oz) stewed tomatoes, drained**
1 can (4oz) chopped green chilies *(Old El Paso)*

2 oz shredded, low moisture, part skim mozzarella cheese

- Soak rice in chicken broth 30 to 45 minutes.
- While rice soaks, put remaining ingredients (all but cheese) in serving dish.
- Add softened rice to vegetable mixture. Stir well.
- Top each serving with a light sprinkling of shredded cheese.

If you are watching your sodium intake, use no-salt tomatoes.

* You can use commercial bulgur in place of instant brown rice, or you can make your own. Instructions for making bulgur are on page 113.
** Save the tomato juice to drink later.

This is a delightful dish that has a wonderful Southwest flavor. I call it "Simply Southwest."

SIMPLY SOUTHWEST

Makes 4 large servings

2 cups instant brown rice*

1 can (14.5oz) chicken broth *(Swanson 1/3 Less Sodium)*

1 small onion, chopped

1 garlic clove, minced

2 cups diced cooked turkey *(Louis Rich Oven Baked)***

2 cups (2 small) thinly sliced zucchini

1 medium red bell pepper, chopped (Use the seeds.)

1 tsp ground cumin

1/2 cup picante sauce *(Pace)*

- Soak rice in broth 30 to 45 minutes.
- While rice soaks, put remaining ingredients in a large serving bowl.
- After rice has softened, serve vegetable mixture over rice.

This dish is so simple and so tasty. The next time you fix it, try a variety of veggies. Experiment and have fun.

---

* You can use commercial bulgur in place of instant brown rice, or you can make your own. Instructions for making bulgur are on page 113.

** You may use leftover cooked chicken or turkey. But if you're in a hurry, turkey breast from the deli is the way to go.

There must be something wrong - this tastes too good to be lowfat, nutritious, and quick! This is 'Chip & Dip' made into a complete meal.

When we think of chips and dip, we automatically think of high fat. Not so in this case. If you like the Mexican flavor, you'll love this dip.

A MEXICAN QUICKIE

Makes 1 serving

1/2 cup refried beans *(Rosarita, No Fat)*

1/4 cup picante sauce *(Pace)*

1 serving tortilla chips, about 20 *(Guiltless Gourmet)*

VEGGIES:

Carrot sticks, cauliflower florets, etc.

It takes virtually no effort to get this meal together. Just open a can of refried beans, put a jar of picante sauce on the table, a bag of tortilla chips, and some raw veggies. What could be simpler! Enjoy!

This meal is brimming with energy. The beans and 'whole' corn tortilla chips provide lots of energy. The raw vegetables provide vitamins and minerals as well as active enzymes.

This meal does not contain vitamin B_{12}. If you want some B_{12}, add some type of animal food, such as a light sprinkling of low moisture, part skim mozzarella cheese.

This Red Bean Chicken Salad is very pretty, tastes good, is low in fat and is quite simple to fix. Just throw it together!

RED BEAN CHICKEN SALAD

Makes 4 cups

1 can (15.5oz) red beans, drained *(Green Giant)*

1 can (5oz) white chicken in water, drained *(Swanson)**

3 large celery ribs, chopped

1 medium tomato, chopped

1 TB cooking oil

1 1/2 TB vinegar

2 TB water

2 tsp dried basil

1/4 tsp salt

Pepper to taste

Fresh spinach, torn in bite-size pieces

- In a medium bown, combine beans, chicken, celery, and tomato.
- In a small bowl, combine oil, vinegar, water, basil, salt & pepper; stir well; add to bean mixture. Stir to mix.
- Serve over fresh spinach leaves.

SERVE WITH THIS:

Whole grain crackers

Extra veggies, if you'd like

*You may certainly use your own cooked chicken - or turkey. Canned chicken or turkey is handy when time is short.

If there's any of this pilaf left over, refrigerate it and eat cold the next day. This dish is wonderful served cold.

QUICK RICE PILAF

Makes 9 cups

> 3 cups instant brown rice*
> 3 cups water
>
> 1/2 cup chopped green onions
> 1/2 cup finely chopped cauliflower
> 1/2 cup finely chopped broccoli
> 1 medium tomato, finely chopped
> 1 1/2 cups frozen peas, thawed
>
> 1/4 cup vinegar
> 1/2 cup cold water
> 1 garlic clove, minced
> 1 pkt Fat Free, Italian Salad Dressing Mix (*Good Seasons*)

- Soak rice in water 30 to 45 minutes.
- While rice soaks, put next 5 ingredients in a large serving bowl.
- In a glass jar with a tight fitting lid, put next four ingredients. Shake well.
- Add softened rice and dressing to vegetable mixture. Stir well.

If you want to add some meat to this dish, go ahead. A small amount of cooked poultry or shrimp would be quite tasty.

---

* You can use commercial bulgur in place of instant brown rice, or you can make your own. Instructions for making bulgur are on page 113.

I cannot describe the fantastic flavor this dish has. You must experience it for yourself! I call it "Chicken Surprise" because the flavor is unusual - but delicious.

CHICKEN SURPRISE

Makes 6 servings

2 cups instant brown rice*

1 can (14.5oz) chicken broth *(Swanson 1/3 Less Sodium)*

1 can (15oz) black beans

1 can (10oz) canned white chicken, drained *(Swanson)***

1/2 cup plain, nonfat yogurt

1/3 cup sliced almonds

2 tsp soy sauce

1/4 tsp pepper

1/4 tsp poultry seasoning

- Soak rice in broth 30 to 45 minutes.
- While rice soaks, combine remaining ingredients in large serving dish.
- Add softened rice to dish. Mix well.

GARNISH: This dish looks great with a bit of green and red garnish.

I like to add tomato wedges and parsley sprigs. Sprinkle a few almond slices over the top. This is pleasing to the eye.

---

* You can use commercial bulgur in place of instant brown rice, or you can make your own. Instructions for making bulgur are on page 113.

** You may certainly use leftover, cooked chicken or turkey. I like to have leftover, cooked poultry available for dishes such as this.

This is a convenient dish to fix because most of these ingredients we can have on hand.

CHICKEN RICE SALAD

Makes 5 to 6 servings

1 cup instant brown rice*
1 cup water

2 TB cooking oil
2 TB fresh lemon juice
1/2 tsp salt
2 celery ribs, chopped
6 green onions, chopped
1 can (10oz) chicken *(Swanson)*
1 tsp poultry seasoning

Garnish:
Lettuce leaves
Tomato wedges

- Soak rice in water 30 to 45 minutes
- Combine remaining ingredients in large bowl.
- Add softened rice. Stir well.

Serve on lettuce leaves with tomato wedges.

Be creative and use different meats; salmon, tuna, or mackerel.

---

* You can use commercial bulgur in place of instant brown rice, or you can make your own. Instructions for making bulgur are on page 113.

Tomatoes make such a colorful presentation, and stuffed tomatoes are especially inviting. If you have access to home grown tomatoes, this will be a superb tasting dish.

CHICKEN STUFFED TOMATOES

Makes 4 servings

4 large, firm tomatoes
1/2 cup wheat germ
1/2 cup chopped green onions
1/2 cup chopped celery
1/2 cup chopped green olives*
1 can (10oz) chicken, drained *(Swanson)*

Garnish:
Lettuce leaves
Avocado slices

• Cut tops off tomatoes.
• Scoop out pulp, leaving shells intact.
• Dice tomato pulp and tops; put in bowl.
• Put remaining ingredients in bowl. Stir to mix.
• Stuff tomatoes with filling.
• Put each tomato on a lettuce leaf.
• Garnish with avacado slices.

* Look for green olives that do not contain sodium alginate or potassium sorbate.

Canned chicken (or turkey) is great to keep on hand for dishes like this one.

SUMMER CHICKEN SALAD

Makes 3 1/2 cups

1 can (5oz) white chicken (*Swanson*)

1 can (8oz) sliced water chestnuts, drained

1/2 bunch green onions, chopped

2 ribs celery, sliced

1 cup chopped tomato

1/2 cup plain, nonfat yogurt*

1/2 tsp dried dill weed

2 TB capers**

Lettuce leaves

• Put all ingredients in mixing bowl. Stir to mix.
• Serve on lettuce leaves.

Serve in whole wheat pita pockets, whole wheat tortillas or with whole grain crackers.

* For a taste change, use fat free sour cream in place of the yogurt.
** Look for capers in the section with olives.

When we think of chili, we think of a hearty flavor that includes chili powder. This chili gets its name from green chilies - not chili powder. The flavor is much milder than that of chili powder. I think you'll like it.

WHITE BEANS & CHICKEN CHILI

Makes 4 to 6 servings

2 cans (14.5oz each) Great Northern Beans, drained*

2 garlic cloves, minced

1 tsp cumin

2 tsp dried oregano

1 can (4.5oz) chopped green chilies

1 green onion, chopped

1/2 cup chopped red bell pepper (Use the seeds.)

1 can (10oz) white chicken, drained *(Swanson)***

• Put all ingredients in serving bowl. Mix well.

Pass the tortilla chips. My favorite chips are Guiltless Gourmet. For more information, see page 73.

* Choose any brand of canned bean that does not contain EDTA.

** Swanson canned chicken does not contain MSG. Many other brands do.

To learn more about harmful additives and preservatives, see *The Food Storage Bible* page 158.

Canned tuna is a great food to keep on hand for dishes like this.

TUNA PILAF

Makes 5 servings

1 cup instant brown rice*
1 can (14.5oz) chicken broth *(Swanson 1/3 Less Sodium)*

2 cups frozen peas, thawed
1/4 cup chopped onion
1 garlic clove, minced
1 medium red bell pepper, chopped (Use the seeds.)
1 can (6.5oz) water pack tuna, drained
Pepper to taste

- Soak rice in broth 30 to 45 minutes.
- While rice soaks, put remaining ingredients in serving dish.
- Add softened rice to mixture. Stir well.

I like to have a slice of whole wheat bread with this meal.

This is a great dish for leftovers. If you have any left over, take some with you to work tomorrow.

* You can use commercial bulgur in place of instant brown rice, or you can make your own. Instructions for making bulgur are on page 113.

This is a very refreshing salad using fruit and tuna. The flavor is unique and very tasty.

TROPICAL TUNA SALAD

Makes 3 servings

3 ripe bananas, sliced

1 can (20oz) pineapple chunks, drained

1 can (6oz) water pack tuna, drained*

1/4 cup chopped celery

3/4 cup plain, nonfat yogurt

2 TB fresh lemon juice

1/4 tsp salt

1/4 cup sliced almonds

Garnish: Red Grapes

- Put first four ingredients in a serving bowl.
- In a separate bowl, mix together yogurt, lemon juice and salt.
- Add yogurt mixture to tuna mixture. Stir to mix.
- Top each serving with sliced almonds.

Garnish with clusters of red grapes.

This is a very attractive main dish salad. It's not only pretty, it's very healthful. Feel good about serving dishes like this to your family.

* You can substitute salmon, mackerel, or chicken for the tuna.

Here is another tasty main dish salad using tuna. Instead of fruit, this salad uses fresh vegetables. I love the flavor of fresh tomatoes and zucchini together. See what you think.

SICILIAN TUNA SALAD

Makes 4 to 5 servings

2 cups chopped, fresh tomatoes

2 cups chopped zucchini

1 can (6oz) water pack tuna, drained*

1 tsp dry dill weed

1/2 tsp salt

1 garlic clove, minced

2 TB fresh lemon juice

Pepper to taste

Lettuce leaves

• Combine all ingredients in a large serving bowl.

Serve on lettuce leaves.

Pass the whole grain crackers.

* The next time you fix this dish, use salmon, mackerel, or cooked or canned chicken or turkey.

These are fun little boats. They're not only fun - they're nutritious! Your children will enjoy helping make - and eat - these little dinghies.

SALMON BOATS

Makes 8 to 10 boats

2 cups firm or extra firm tofu*

1 envelope *Lipton Onion Soup Mix*

2 tsp fresh lemon juice

1 cup drained, canned salmon

2 TB salmon liquid

2 green onions, chopped

1/2 cup chopped celery

8 - 10 hard, whole grain dinner rolls

- In blender or food processor, blend until smooth: tofu, soup mix, lemon juice and salmon liquid.
- Put mixture in bowl; add salmon, onions, and celery. Mix well.
- Cut tops from rolls. Pull out bread leaving crust to form a "boat".
- Fill each boat with salmon mixture.

Pass the veggies:

Carrot sticks, cauliflower florets, cucumber slices, etc.

Kids really do like these little boats. They like helping make them as well as eating them. Just don't tell them they're eating tofu!

Be creative, and use boats for all sorts of fillings.

---

* For a different taste, use fat free sour cream.

If you're a shrimp lover, you'll like this main dish salad. The flavor is delightful with the mixture of citrus, shrimp and onions.

SHRIMP & BROWN RICE SALAD

Makes 5 to 6 servings

1 cup instant brown rice*
1 cup water

2 TB cooking oil
2 TB fresh lemon juice
1 TB grated orange peel
1/2 tsp salt
2 oranges, coarsely chopped
3 green onions, chopped
2 cans (4.5oz each) shrimp, drained (*Chicken of the Sea*)

Garnish:
Lettuce leaves
Tomato wedges

- Soak rice in water 30 to 45 minutes.
- Combine remaining ingredients in large bowl.
- Add softened rice. Stir well.

Serve on lettuce leaves with tomato wedges as garnish.

The brown rice makes this a hearty salad, but the flavor is light with the combination of shrimp and orange pieces.

---

* You can use commercial bulgur in place of instant brown rice, or you can make your own. Instructions for making bulgur are on page 113.

You know my opinion of fresh fruits and vegetables - they're very important! Sometimes it's difficult to eat fresh vegetables everyday. So, here is a very simple recipe that includes a variety of fresh vegetables. If your family doesn't care for the veggies I've chosen, use the ones you like.

Keep this dish readily available in the fridge.

VEGETABLE MEDLEY

Makes 5 servings

> 2 cups frozen peas, thawed
>
> 2 cups frozen corn, thawed
>
> 2 cups chopped tomatoes
>
> 1 cup broccoli florets
>
> 1 cup sliced, fresh mushrooms
>
> 2 ribs celery, sliced
>
> 1/2 cup chopped onion
>
> Shredded, low moisture, part skim mozzarella
> cheese (optional)
>
> FAT FREE DRESSING
> 1 cup water
>
> 2 TB vinegar
>
> 1 garlic clove, minced
>
> 1 pkt Italian Fat Free Dressing Mix *(Good Seasons)*

- Put peas and corn in large serving bowl.
- Add remaining vegetables.
- Put dressing ingredients in a container with a tight fitting lid.

VEGETABLE MEDLEY (Cont'd)

- Shake vigorously until well mixed.
- Add dressing to vegetable mixture; stir.

This dish is a complete protein. The peas (a legume) and the corn (a grain) form a complete protein.

If you want to add a bit of cheese for vitamin B_{12}, go right ahead. Just use a small amount.

This main dish is light, refreshing, and very tasty. Use leftover cooked chicken or turkey, or use canned chicken or turkey. I like to have leftover poultry for dishes such as this.

CHICKEN SALAD WITH A TWIST

Makes 5 1/2 cups

> 1 cup instant brown rice*
> 1 cup water
>
> 1 can (10oz) chicken, drained well *(Sweet Sue)***
> 1 bag (6oz) radishes, sliced
> 2 medium oranges cut in bite size pieces
> 2/3 cup honey-mustard dressing *(Pritikin)*
>
> Lettuce leaves

- Soak rice in water 30 to 45 minutes
- In serving bowl, combine remaining ingredients.
- Add softened rice to serving bowl. Stir well.
- Serve on lettuce leaves.

Pass the whole grain crackers. (One of my favorite whole grain crackers is Toasted Sesame Rye by Ryvita. Most stores carry this brand.)

---

* You can use commercial bulgur in place of instant brown rice, or you can make your own. Instructions for making bulgur are on page 113.

** Choose brands of canned chicken or turkey that don't contain MSG. For more information about harmful additives and preservatives, see *The Food Storage Bible* page 158.

What a hearty, main dish salad!

BLACK BEAN & BROWN RICE SALAD

Makes 4 1/2 cups

1 cup instant brown rice*

1 cup water

1 can (15oz) black beans, drained

1/2 cup lowfat cottage cheese**

1/2 cup chopped green onion

1/4 cup picante sauce (Pace)

- Soak rice in water 30 to 45 minutes
- In serving bowl, combine remaining ingredients.
- Add softened rice to serving bowl. Stir well to mix.

This dish is a complete protein without the cottage cheese. The beans, (a legume) and the rice (a grain) make this a complete protein. By adding cottage cheese, we've added vitamin B_{12}.

* You can use commercial bulgur in place of instant brown rice, or you can make your own. Instructions for making bulgur are on page 113.

** If you are sensitive to dairy, substitute tofu for cottage cheese. Also, when purchasing cottage cheese, choose brands without polysorbates and potassium sorbate.

This dish is good as a main dish or as a side dish.

BEAN & CHEESE SALAD

Makes 3 servings

> 1 can pinto beans*
>
> 1 medium onion, finely chopped
>
> 2 medium tomatoes, chopped
>
> 2 oz shredded, low moisture, part skim mozzarella cheese
>
> 2 tsp chopped fresh parsley
>
> Pepper to taste
>
> Vinaigrette dressing
>
> VINAIGRETTE DRESSING
>
> 2 TB cooking oil
>
> 1/4 cup rice vinegar**
>
> 1 garlic clove, minced
>
> 1 TB Dijon mustard
>
> 1 1/2 tsp dried oregano leaves
>
> 1/4 tsp salt
>
> Dash pepper

- In serving bowl, mix salad ingredients.
- In small bowl, combine dressing ingredients; add to salad.
- Stir well to mix.

This is such a simple, yet tasty, dish. Keep the ingredients on hand and serve often.

---

* Choose a brand of pinto beans that does not contain EDTA. EDTA pulls valuable metals from the body - metals such as iron, zinc, calcium, and others. For more information about additives and preservatives, see *The Food Storage Bible* page 158.

** Choose vinegar that doesn't contain sulfites. People with allergies and/or asthma can be highly sensitive to sulfites.

This main dish salad is very tasty and is low in fat - unlike its regular counterpart. If you like Waldorf Salad, you'll love this lowfat version made with brown rice.

BROWN RICE WALDORF SALAD

Makes 8, one cup servings

1 cup instant brown rice*
1 cup water

4 medium red apples, diced (Do not peel.)
2 TB fresh lemon juice
2 TB apple juice concentrate
3 celery ribs, thinly sliced (1 1/2 cups)
1/2 cup chopped pecans
1/2 cup dark raisins
1 cup plain, nonfat yogurt
1/2 tsp cinnamon
1/4 tsp nutmeg
1/4 tsp allspice

- Soak rice in water 30 to 45 minutes.
- While rice soaks, chop apples into a serving bowl.
- Add lemon juice. Stir well.
- Add remaining ingredients.
- Stir in softened rice.

You can use regular brown rice in this dish, but it will need to be cooked.

* You can also use commercial bulgur in place of instant brown rice, or you can make your own. Instructions for making bulgur are on page 113.

BULGUR

I love the taste and texture of bulgur. It is simple to make if you have whole wheat berries and a grinder. (You can also make instant brown rice using this same method.)

You can use either a hand mill or an electric mill to grind your berries.

Note: To make bulgur, or instant brown rice, you must first crack your grain, then heat to boiling. This is the only recipe in this book that requires cooking. But if you want to make your own bulgur, or instant brown rice, you can do it if you have a heat source.

PREPARE GRAIN

• Put whole wheat berries, or brown rice, in your mill and grind just enough to crack the berries.

• Sift the cracked grain to remove flour and small particles.*

TO MAKE BULGUR
OR INSTANT BROWN RICE

1 cup cracked wheat, or cracked brown rice

1 3/4 cups water

• Put cracked grain and water in saucepan.

• Bring to a full boil; cover; and turn off heat.

• Let set 15 minutes or until water is absorbed.

Now you have bulgur or instant brown rice! I like to make a large batch, and then freeze what I don't use in zip lock bags. By doing this, I have bulgur and instant brown rice available whenever I need it.

* These very fine grain particles are called "Farina" and are similar to Cream of Wheat® or Cream of Rice®.

NOTE: This information was taken from *Natural Meals In Minutes* by Rita Bingham. For more information about her books, see pages 159 and 160.

For more recipes using wheat, see *The Amazing Wheat Book* by LeArta Moulton, page 161.

SIDE DISHES

Side dishes can spice up a meal. They can add color and pizazz as well as provide valuable nutrients.

Remember that salads and soups make wonderful side dishes. For Salads, see page 29. For Soups, see page 23.

This side dish can be prepared anytime of year as tomatoes are available all year. But, if you have 'home grown' tomatoes, this dish will be much more flavorful. (I'm sure it will have more nutrients as well!)

TOMATO - BASIL BRUSCHETTA

Makes 5 cups

> 3 medium tomatoes, chopped
>
> 1 bunch green onions, chopped
>
> 3 tsp dried basil*
>
> 1 garlic clove, minced
>
> 1/2 tsp salt
>
> Dash of pepper

- Combine all ingredients in a serving bowl. Mix well.

Serve immediately or refrigerate to serve later.

---

* If you have fresh basil, definitely use it. There is no comparison between the flavor of fresh herbs and dried.

Have you ever been to a baked potato bar? You are served a baked potato, then you choose the topping for your potato from the many side dishes that are available.

This is one of my favorite baked potato toppings.

EL SOMBRERO BAKED POTATO TOPPING

Makes 1 cup

1 cup plain, nonfat yogurt

2 TB *Molly McButter Cheese Dairy Sprinkles*

2 TB chopped, canned jalapeños

1 green onion, chopped

1/2 tsp cumin

1/4 tsp chili powder

• Mix all ingredients together.

• Pour into a serving dish.

If you like a hotter topping, use more jalapeños - or use fresh jalapeños.

This is a hearty side dish that provides abundant energy because of the brown rice.

ALMOND RICE PILAF

Makes 5 cups

1 cup instant brown rice*

1 can (14.5oz) chicken broth *(Swanson 1/3 Less Sodium)*

1/2 cup chopped green onion

1/2 cup sliced almonds

- Soak rice in broth 30 to 45 minutes.
- Add onions and almonds. Stir well.

This is a great side dish served with your choice of meat. Or use this dish as part of a vegetarian meal substituting vegetable broth for chicken broth.

* You can use commercial bulgur in place of instant brown rice, or you can make your own. Instructions for making bulgur are on page 113.

DIPS

Most dips are *very* high in fat, and many commercial dips contain harmful additives and preservatives.

These dips on the following pages are *very* nutritious, they're low in fat, and they have no harmful additives or preservatives. AND, they're *very* tasty.

When we combine the right ingredients, dips can even be a complete meal. Some of my favorite lunches consist of dips and their trimmings. Do give these a try. I think your family will love them.

One of the most popular dips is a spinach dip. It is not only tasty, it's nutritious.

SAVORY SPINACH DIP

Makes about 2 cups

1 pkg (10oz) frozen <u>chopped</u> spinach, thawed
1 pkg (12.3oz) *Mori-Nu Lite Tofu*, firm or extra firm*
1 envelope *Lipton Savory Herb with Garlic Soup Mix*

- Squeeze liquid from spinach.
- Put all ingredients in blender or food processor.
- Blend until smooth.

Pass the whole grain crackers.

What a great way to get phytoestrogen! You see, tofu is a great source of plant estrogen.

By the way, you'll never know you're eating tofu!

* For a different taste and texture, use fat free sour cream in place of the tofu.

Here is another version of the popular spinach dip.

SAVORY SPINACH & WATER CHESTNUT DIP

Makes 3 cups

1 pkg (12.3oz) *Mori-Nu Lite Tofu*, firm or extra firm

1 pkt *Lipton Onion Soup Mix*

1/2 cup fat free sour cream*

1 to 3 large garlic cloves**

1 pkg (10oz) frozen, <u>chopped</u> spinach, thawed

1 can (8oz) water chestnuts, drained

2 green onions, chopped

- In food processor or blender, blend first four ingredients.
- Squeeze moisture from thawed spinach; add to blender, and blend.
- Add water chestnuts and onions. Blend just until chestnuts are chopped into small pieces.

Serve immediately, or chill for later.

Serve with bite size veggies and/or whole grain crackers.

This is a very tasty, nutritious, lowfat dip. Be prepared to share the recipe. (No one will believe this is made with tofu!)

* Choose fat free sour cream that does not contain potassium sorbate, artificial color, or artificial flavor.

** If you want a hot dip, use three garlic cloves; otherwise, stick with one.

If you like artichokes, you'll love this dip.

ARTICHOKE DIP

Makes 2 cups

      1 can (14oz) artichoke hearts, in water

      1 1/2 cups fat free sour cream *(Daisy)**

      1 envelope *Lipton Onion Soup Mix*

- Finely chop artichoke hearts.
- Put chopped artichokes, sour cream and soup mix in bowl.
- Stir to mix well.

Serve with whole grain crackers, or veggies such as;
Carrot sticks, celery sticks, cucumber slices, etc.

* Choose fat free sour cream that does not contain potassium sorbate, artificial color, or artificial flavor.

This is a terrific dip with Mexican flavor.

This mixture is also great as a topping for baked potatoes. Many times I will have a baked potato with this topping for lunch - along with some raw veggies.

SOUTH OF THE BORDER DIP

Makes 1 cup

1 cup plain, nonfat yogurt

2 TB *Molly McButter Cheese Dairy Sprinkles*

2 TB chopped, canned jalapeños

1 green onion, chopped

1/2 tsp cumin

1/4 tsp chili powder

• Mix all ingredients well.
• Serve with baked tortilla chips.

If you like a hotter dip, use more jalapeños.

My favorite tortilla chips? My favorite by far are the many varieties by Guiltless Gourmet. Most grocery stores carry the Guiltless Gourmet brand. (Don't you just love that name?) If your store doesn't have them, look in a health food store. If you still can't find them, call the company in Austin, Texas: 1-800-723-9541.

I assure you, it is worth the effort to get these chips. They are wonderful! I buy them by the case!

How about another flavorful Mexican dip? This dip is soooo simple. Give it a try. I bet you'll like it.

FIESTA DIP

Makes 1 cup

1 cup lowfat cottage cheese, drained

2 TB mild picante sauce *(Pace)**

- In a blender or mixer, combine ingredients; blend until smooth.

Pass the tortilla chips. My favorite are Guiltless Gourmet.

See page 73.

* If you like a hot dip, use a hot picante sauce. If you like a *really* hot dip, add a finely chopped, fresh jalapeño.

Bean dips are very popular. Our grocery shelves are well stocked with this dip. Instead of buying a bean dip, let's make our own - from scratch.

MONTEREY BEAN DIP

Makes about 3 cups

2 cans Great Northern Beans, drained *(Bush's)*

1/4 cup reserved bean juice

1 envelope *Lipton Onion Soup Mix*

1 tsp dried parsley flakes

1 TB fresh lemon juice

1 garlic clove

1/4 tsp pepper

1/3 cup medium picante sauce *(Pace)*

- Put all ingredients in blender or food processor.
- Blend until smooth.

Pass the tortilla chips.

This is a complete protein with the combination of a legume (beans) and a grain (corn tortilla chips). To make this a complete meal, just add some raw veggies.

This dip is my absolute favorite! Many times I will make this dip just for myself. (I will share if there are other people around!)

DON'T TELL 'EM & THEY'LL NEVER KNOW!! If you don't tell, no one will know they're eating tofu. This dip is soooo good - and it's nutritious.

It takes very little effort to throw this together. Fix it and keep it in the fridge for those kids who are always hungry.

VEGGIE DIP

Makes 2 cups

1 pkg (12.3oz) *Mori-Nu Lite Tofu*, firm or extra firm

1 1/2 tsp fresh lemon juice

1 garlic clove

2 TB diced onion

1 TB dried cilantro

1 cup frozen peas, thawed

1/2 tsp salt

1 small tomato, diced

- In a blender or food processor, combine first seven ingredients.
- Blend until smooth.
- Put mixture in a serving bowl.
- Stir in diced tomatoes.

Serve this dip with Guiltless Gourmet corn chips. (See page 73.)

With corn chips, this dip is a complete protein. The corn (a grain) and the peas and tofu (legumes), make this a complete protein.

I do hope you give this a try. I think you'll love it.

This is a very tasty spread for crackers, and it makes a great dip. The flavor is unique and very good. It's a tasty way to get soy in your diet. (You won't even know this is made with tofu!) Do give this one a try.

DILLED SHRIMP DIP

Makes 1 1/4 cups

1/4 cup skim milk (or low fat soy milk)

1 tsp fresh lemon juice

1/2 tsp Worcestershire sauce

1 <u>small</u> garlic clove

1/4 tsp dried dill weed

1 cup firm tofu

1 can (4.5 oz) shrimp, rinsed & chopped*

- In a blender or food processor, blend all ingredients but shrimp.
- Put mixture in a serving dish. Stir in shrimp.

If you're wanting an elegant presentation, serve in a shell-shaped dish with whole shrimp for garnish. Offer a variety of whole grain crackers on the side.

This spread is even better after it has chilled for at least an hour. Shrimp lovers will love this one!

* You may use fresh or frozen, cooked shrimp.

Shrimp is great to use in dips. Here's another variation of a great tasting shrimp dip.

SHRIMP & HERB DIP

Makes 2 1/2 cups

2 cups tofu, firm or extra firm*

1 envelope *Lipton Savory Herb with Garlic Soup Mix*

1 can (4.5 oz) shrimp *(Chicken of the Sea)*

Parsley for garnish

- In blender or food processor, blend tofu and soup mix until smooth.
- Chop shrimp, saving a few whole shrimp for garnish.
- Put shrimp and tofu mixture in serving bowl and mix well.
- Garnish with shrimp and fresh parsley sprigs.

Pass the whole grain crackers.

* For a different taste, substitute fat free sour cream for the tofu.

Tuna is another seafood that makes a great dip. Give this one a try.

TUNA DIP

Makes about 2 cups

1 1/2 cups lowfat cottage cheese*

1 can (6oz) water pack tuna, drained

1 tsp fresh lemon juice

1 tsp dried parsley

- In blender or mixer, blend cottage cheese until smooth.
- In a serving bowl, combine blended cheese and remaining ingredients.
- Stir well to mix.

SERVE WITH:

Whole grain crackers

Raw veggies

* Choose a cottage cheese that does not contain polysorbates or potassium sorbate.

SAUCES

Sauces can enhance the flavor of foods and make them exquisite. And sauces can also cover up an inferior cut of meat.

We can make sauces unique with subtle flavorings by the spices we use. It is exciting to create a new, unique sauce that compliments a dish.

We are familiar with common sauces such as spaghetti sauce, pizza sauce, tartar sauce, and so on. But let's be creative and fix some that are not so common.

This cocktail sauce is great for shrimp and other seafood. I like this sauce much better than the cocktail sauces available on our grocery shelves. This one is a favorite at our house. I hope it will be a favorite at yours, too.

SEAFOOD COCKTAIL SAUCE

Makes 1 1/2 cups

    1 bottle (12oz) chili sauce

    1 TB fresh lemon juice

    1 tsp Worcestershire sauce

    1 to 2 TBS prepared horseradish*

    1/4 tsp salt

    Pepper to taste

• Mix all ingredients.

Use immediately, or chill for later.

* If you want a hot cocktail sauce, use 2 tablespoons horseradish. If not, stick with one tablespoon. (You will find prepared horseradish in the refrigerated section of your grocery store.)

Do you like pasta? At our house, we *love* pasta! At home, we eat only whole wheat pasta. Some restaurants now serve whole wheat pasta and of course, these are the restaurants where we eat.

If you haven't had whole wheat pasta, I certainly recommend you try it. It not only tastes much better than the white 'stuff', it is much more nutritious.

Pasta was made for a variety of sauces. The following sauce is sooooo simple, yet it gives us a very tasty pasta sauce that's also very good for us.

I'm always looking for ways to incorporate tofu in meals. But for me, tofu must be camouflaged because I don't care for its taste. This sauce is very creamy and has a marvelous taste. You would never know this sauce contains tofu. Just don't tell your friends and family. They'll never know!!

CREAMY PASTA SAUCE

Makes 2 cups

1 can (15oz) Ready Tomato Sauce *(Hunt's)*

1 cup firm or extra firm tofu

- Put ingredients in a blender; blend until smooth.
- Put sauce in a bowl and microwave until hot.

Serve over any whole grain pasta.

If you are sensitive to wheat, there is corn, brown rice and spelt pasta. Be aware that some people who are sensitive to wheat are also sensitive to spelt. You can find these varieties of pasta at health food stores and some grocery stores.

If you are a roast beef or lamb lover and like a tasty sauce for your meat, give this sauce a try.

HORSERADISH SAUCE

Makes 1/2 cup

> 1/2 cup fat free sour cream *(Daisy)**
> 1 TB drained, prepared horseradish
> Dash of salt

- Combine all ingredients. Stir well to mix.

Serve over roasted beef or lamb.

---

* When purchasing sour cream, look for those without potassium sorbate, artificial color, and artificial flavor.

Here is another tasty sauce for meats. This sauce goes particularly well with roast pork and lamb.

HONEY MUSTARD SAUCE

Makes about 1 cup

1/2 cup Dijon mustard

1/2 cup honey

1 tsp salt

1/2 tsp dried tarragon

1/4 tsp pepper

- Combine all ingredients. Stir well to mix.
- Baste meat during last half of cooking period.
- Just before serving, top meat with remaining sauce.

Basting during the last half of cooking gives a tangy-sweet flavor to the meat. Many people like a sweet and sour taste on meat.

These butter sauces are quite simple to make, and if you're a butter lover, these different flavored butters are delightful.

QUICK BUTTER SAUCES*

Soften 1/4 cup butter then add one of the following:

Almond butter:	Add 1 TB chopped toasted almonds
Caper butter:	Add 1 TB minced capers.
Celery seed butter:	Add 1 tsp celery seed.
Curry butter:	Add 1/4 tsp curry powder.
Dilly butter:	Add 1 tsp dried dill weed.
Garlic butter:	Add 1/2 minced garlic clove.
Horseradish butter:	Add 1 /2 tsp prepared horseradish.
Lemon butter:	Add 1 tsp grated lemon peel and 1 TB juice.
Mustard butter:	Add 2 tsp German mustard.
Onion butter:	Add 1 TB finely chopped onion.
Parmesan butter:	Add 1 1/2 TB grated parmesan cheese.
Poppy seed butter:	Add 1 tsp poppy seed and 1 TB lemon juice.

- Soften butter; add flavor of choice.
- Stir to mix well.

If the butter and flavoring are allowed to set for a couple hours, the flavor will be more intense.

These are excellent flavors to use with steamed vegetables, some are great spread on whole grain breads and whole grain crackers, and some are good on seafood, beef, pork, and lamb.

Try different flavors to see what your family enjoys.

* For my favorite butter mix, see the next page.

Many times I'm asked, "Which is better, butter or margarine?" Butter is the better choice. But I have a mix that I think is better than either butter or margarine. I call it my butter mix. You can now call it your butter mix.

JAYNE'S BUTTER MIX

1 pound butter, lightly salted

2 cups cold pressed, sunflower oil*

- Put butter in blender and let set at room temperature until soft.
- Add oil. Blend until smooth.
- Put in covered containers and refrigerate.

This mix will taste soooo good you may be tempted to overeat it. Remember this is 100% fat, so use it sparingly.

By making this mix, you now have half the saturated fat and half the cholesterol of butter. (Butter has very little cholesterol to begin with.)

The important thing is that this mix does not contain trans-fatty acids. Trans-fats are found in margarines. The body cannot tolerate trans-fats, and one thing scientists know for certain, trans-fatty acids destroy HDLs (good cholesterol) and increase LDLs (bad cholesterol).

In addition to trans-fatty acids, most margarines contain (ethylenediamine tetra-acetic acid) EDTA. EDTA is a chelating agent and as such, pulls metals from the body; metals such as iron, zinc, copper, CALCIUM, and others.

For more informatin about harmful additives and preservatives in foods, see *The Food Storage Bible* page 158.

---

* I use cold pressed sunflower oil as it contains more vitamin E than most cooking oils.

DESSERTS

Most of us like the sweet taste of desserts. This includes me!

We are accustomed to the high fat, refined sugar, and refined flour taste found in many of our prepared desserts. The desserts found here will not have this taste - but they still taste very good.

You can feel good about serving these desserts to your family.

CHOCOLATE LOVERS...

If you like chocolate, I think you'll really like this dessert.

This mousse is not as rich or sweet as mousse made with fat and refined sugar, but it's still *very* good.

Just a hint: Don't tell anyone this is made with tofu. (I bet no one will be able to tell!)

CHOCOLATE MOUSSE

Makes 5 cups

1 cup apple juice concentrate

1/4 cup cocoa powder*

2 pkgs (12.3 oz each) *Mori-Nu Lite Tofu*, firm or extra firm

1 TB vanilla

2 ripe bananas, sliced

Sliced almonds

- In blender or food processor, blend first four ingredients.
- Put mixture in serving dishes.
- Stir in banana slices, saving a few for garnish.
- Garnish each serving with banana slices and sliced almonds.

This is so tasty, I frequently fix it just for me!

This is a great way to get estrogen in the diet. The soybean is an excellent source of plant estrogen. And tofu is made from soybeans.

NOTE: This recipe is simple to cut in half.

* Carob powder, which does not contain caffeine, can be used in place of cocoa powder.

Kids, as well as adults, love gelatin desserts. And they can be healthful - if the right ingredients are used. They're simple to fix, fat free and sugar free - again, if we use the right ingredients.

Most all gelatin desserts contain artificial colors and artificial flavors. The sugar free gelatins also contain aspartame. For good health, these are all ingredients that should be avoided.

With this recipe, we use the microwave to heat the juice. But we don't dirty a pan!

GELATIN DESSERT

Makes 4 servings

2 cups juice*

1 pkt *Knox Unflavored Gelatine*

2 bananas, sliced (or other fruit)

- Put 1/2 cup juice in a serving bowl; add gelatin to soften.
- Microwave remaining 1 1/2 cups juice to boiling; add to gelatin mixture; stir well.
- Add 2 sliced bananas, or other fruit.
- Refrigerate until set.

My family likes gelatin desserts made with grape juice as well as Welch's White Grape Classics such as White Grape Raspberry. Be creative, and use different juices and different fruits.

NOTES:

1. Don't use fresh or frozen pineapple. The live enzyme, bromelain, keeps gelatin from congealing.

2. Use white grape juices that do not contain sulfites. For more about harmful additives and preservatives, see *The Food Storage Bible*, page 158.

* Use 100% fruit juices - not juice cocktails etc. which contain sugar.

Are you a cheesecake lover? Cheesecakes are very popular, and they are also very high in fat. A typical small piece of cheesecake has approximately 25 grams of fat. This recipe is virtually fat free because it is made with fat free cream cheese.

Change the flavor of this recipe by using different fruit jams.

STRAWBERRY CHEESECAKE

Makes 8 servings

1 prepared graham cracker crust*

1 envelope *Knox Unflavored Gelatine*

1/2 cup strawberry jam**

1 cup boiling water

2 pkgs (8oz each) Fat Free Cream Cheese,
softened *(Healthy Choice)*

- In a large mixing bowl, stir gelatin into the jam. Let set for a couple minutes.
- In microwave, heat 1/2 cup water to boiling. Stir into jam mixture until gelatin is completely dissolved.
- Add softened cream cheese and beat until smooth.
- Pour into prepared crust.
- Garnish with spoonfuls of jam dropped around top edge of cheesecake.
- Chill.

* You can make your own graham cracker crust using Health Valley, Animal Graham Crackers. These are whole wheat, fat free graham crackers. (Besides being great for a crust, they're super snacks for kids.)

** Use jams that are made with only fruit and fruit juices. Look for such brands as Polaner and Smucker's Simply Fruit.

Creamy puddings are delightful. They're even better when we know they're nutritious. Here's one that is both tasty and healthful.

BANANA CREAM PUDDING

Makes 1 1/2 cups

1 cup lowfat cottage cheese

1 ripe banana

1/4 cup apple juice concentrate

1 ripe banana

• Put first three ingredients in blender; blend until smooth.
• Slice extra banana; stir into blended mixture.

Pass some homemade whole grain cookies - or Health Valley whole grain cookies.

SPROUTS

Sprouts are some of the most healthful foods we have. A seed is the life force of a plant. When moisture is added to a seed, that seed comes to life, producing abundant energy and nutrients for the new plant. When we eat newly sprouted seeds, we receive abundant energy and nutrients.

From sprouts we get, vitamins, minerals, antioxidants, phytochemicals (plant chemicals), and active enzymes. In fact, we get many times more of these nutrients from freshly sprouted seeds than we get from fruits and vegetables! Fresh sprouts are powerhouses!

Have you ever thought where we would get the majority of our nutrients and active enzymes if there were no fresh fruits and vegetables available? All we have to do is sprout seeds!

I always have seeds on hand to sprout. I sprout seeds regularly to put in salads, sandwiches, etc. Also, by having seeds on hand, I know I'll always have the source for nutrients and active enzymes if fresh food is not available.

Since enzymes and some vitamins, such as vitamin C, are sensitive to air and light, it is best to sprout a small amount of seeds every few days instead of a large amount that will be exposed to air and light over a period of time.

Fresh Seeds

When sprouting, use fresh seeds as fresh seeds germinate better than older seeds. This means that if you are storing seeds, you should use them and rotate them.

How Much To Store

When there are no fresh fruits or vegetables available, it is recommended that each adult get a *minimum* of 1/2 cup sprouted seeds daily. (Approximately 2 tablespoons of seeds equals 1/2 cup sprouted seeds. The size of the seed determines the volume.) This means that approximately 2 1/2 pounds of seeds should be stored for one adult for one month. Store a varitey of seeds for sprouting. This will provide a variety of taste as well as a variety of nutrients.

Common Sprouting Seeds

Any seed that makes a plant can be sprouted, but some are more available and easier to sprout than others. Below is a list of some favorites:

Alfalfa	All Legumes:
Buckwheat	Kidney beans
Clover	Lentils
Radish	Mung beans
Sunflower	Pea, green & blackeye
Wheat	Pinto beans
Barley	Soybeans
Rye	Garbanzos

Balanced Sprouting Mix

I have developed a sprouting mix that contains a balance of grains and legumes. This mixture is a complete protein and supplies an abundance of vitamins, minerals, phytochemicals, antioxidants and active enzymes.

This mix is **NATURE'S BEST Balanced Sprouting Mix.** It contains: Rye, Barley, Green Peas, Green Lentils, Garbanzos, Adzukis, and Radish. This sprouting mix can be ordered from Country Store. See page 156.

Where To Store Seeds

Seeds should be stored in a cool, dry place in air-tight containers.

Ready To Sprout?

The chart below gives you approximate amounts of various seeds, sprouting times, and the yields.

TYPE	AMOUNT	SOAKING TIME	SPROUTING TIME	YIELD
Small seeds:				
Alfalfa, clover, etc	2 TB	4 hrs	5 - 7 days	2 cups
Medium seeds:				
Wheat, Sunflower:	1/2 c	10-12 hrs	2-3 days	1 1/2 cups
Large seeds:				
Soy, Kidney,				
Pinto, etc.	1 c	10-12 hrs	5-6 days	4 cups

Prepare Seeds To Sprout

Before sprouting, sort seeds. Remove broken seeds and pieces of debris.

Ready? Let's Sprout!

Place your seeds in a quart jar. (Or use a seed sprouter. See **Ready Foods 2000**, page 157.) Rinse your sorted seeds. Since "city" water contains chlorine, use purified water for rinsing and soaking seeds. Put a cheese cloth or nylon netting on jar opening and fasten with a jar ring or rubber band. Pour out rinse water then add soaking water - using twice as much water as seeds. Example: to 1/2 cup seeds, use 1 cup water.

After the recommended soaking time (see chart above), pour off soaking water and place jar upside down and slightly tipped so seeds will drain well. (Most sprouting failures occur because seeds were not drained well.)

Rinse seeds with water once each day until sprouts have reached the desired length. (Usually as long as the seed itself.)

Note: The soaking water contains valuable nutrients. So use it when making soups, cooking rice, oatmeal, and so on.

Ready To Eat!

Now, enjoy these yummy sprouts! Some sprouts are better than others to eat plain. (My favorites to eat plain are lentil, garbanzo, and wheat sprouts.)

Sprouts are good in vegetable salads. Also add them to sandwiches, wraps, pocket sandwiches, omelets, and even on top of your favorite soup.

If someone in your family isn't fond of sprouts, blend them in smoothies. They'll never know they've just eaten sprouts! (But their body will know!)

Storing Sprouts

Sprouts are like any fresh food, they begin to lose nutrients in a few days. So use them as soon as possible and store what isn't eaten in a covered container with a paper towel on the bottom and between layers of sprouts. Use within 4 to 5 days.

This is a great tasting sandwich whether it's open-faced or closed! But this sandwich is very appealing when it's served open-faced with sprouts on top.

OPEN-FACED DILLY SANDWICH WITH SPROUTS

Makes 1/2 cup

1/2 cup Tofu Mayonnaise Spread

1/2 tsp dried dill weed

Alfalfa and/or radish sprouts*

TOFU MAYONNAISE SPREAD:

Makes about 2 cups

1 pkg (12.3oz) *Mori-Nu Lite Tofu*, firm or extra firm

1 1/2 TB fresh lemon juice

1 1/2 TB cooking oil

1/2 tsp. salt

- Put Tofu Mayo ingredients in blender, and blend until smooth.
- For Dilly Sandwich, put 1/2 cup mixture in bowl.
- Add dill weed and stir well.
- Put sandwich spread on whole grain bread or whole grain crackers.
- Top with sprouts.

* If you're not familiar with sprouts, I encourage you to try them. Once you have tried sprouting, I think you will want to continue. It's also great fun for children, and they're much more likely to eat sprouts if they have helped sprout the seeds.

Sprouts are great to add to all varieties of slaw salads. Here is one I think you'll like.

RED CABBAGE & SPROUT COLESLAW

Makes 5 cups

3 cups shredded red cabbage

1 cup drained, crushed pineapple

1 cup sprouted wheat or rye

2 cups Best Fruit Dressing

DRESSING:

2 cups low fat cottage cheese*

2 ripe bananas

1/4 cup orange juice

- Put cabbage, pineapple and sprouts in serving bowl.
- Put dressing ingredients in a blender; blend until smooth.
- Add dressing to cabbage mixture. Stir and serve.

This is a very pretty salad and it tastes great! It is so satisfying to have a dish that looks and tastes good and is healthful as well.

* Choose cottage cheese that does not contain polysorbates or potassium sorbate.

Want a fantastic tasting fruit salad that's brimming with nutrients? Give this one a try!

JAMAICAN SALAD

Makes about 3 cups

1 large, ripe banana, sliced

1 large mango, sliced

1/2 cup plain, nonfat yogurt

1/2 cup sprouted wheat or rye

1/4 cup shredded coconut*

• Put all ingredients in serving bowl. Stir and serve.

This truly is a fantastic salad. I hope your family enjoys this one.

* Use shredded coconut that does not contain sulfites

When strawberries are in season, give this salad a try. (If they're not in season, use frozen berries - without sugar.)

STRAWBERRIES & CREAM

Makes about 2 cups

1 large, ripe banana, sliced

1 cup sliced strawberries

1/2 cup sprouted wheat or rye

1/2 cup nonfat sour cream *(Daisy)**

- Put all ingredients in serving bowl. Stir and serve.

This is such a simple salad to throw together. Just have sprouts available, and this dish is a snap!

* If you do not find Daisy brand fat free sour cream, look for brands that do not contain potassium sorbate, artificial color, or artificial flavor.

ABOUT THE AUTHOR...

JAYNE BENKENDORF

CURRENT ACTIVITIES:

Owner - *MEALS IN MINUTES*

A company dedicated to bringing the latest information concerning healthful food and healthy lifestyle to the public.

Author - *THE FOOD STORAGE BIBLE*

A book which lists food products, by brand name, to use and store that are free of harmful additives and preservatives. Each product is coded for fat, sodium, sugar, cholesterol, and overprocessing.

15 MINUTE STORAGE MEALS;
QUICK, HEALTHFUL RECIPES
& FOOD STORAGE HANDBOOK

Quick, healthful, lowfat meals for the person who doesn't have much time to spend in the kitchen. This book also tells how much to store for one month using recipes from this book.

THE NO-COOK COOKBOOK;
NO POTS & PANS TO SCRUB!

If you have no time to cook, if you don't like to cook, or if you have no heat source, this book is for you! Recipes include main meals, side dishes, salads, soups, desserts, and more.

NEVER GO HUNGRY

This audio cassette tells why diets don't work and instructs the listener how to make simple lifestyle changes for weight control and optimum health.

EATING IN RESTAURANTS

This audio cassette tells how to order and what to order for good health when eating in restaurants.

Speaker - MEALS IN MINUTES

Jayne travels nationally giving seminars on choosing healthful food for healthy living and demonstrating that you can get healthful meals on the table in 15 minutes or less.

PAST ACTIVITIES –

Registered Medical Technologist -
Phlebotomist and Clinical Technician

Researcher -
Oklahoma State University School of Veterinary Medicine

Publisher and Editor -
"The Companion" -
A monthly newsletter promoting wellness

Counselor - Weight control and meal planning

Certified Fitness Instructor - Aerobics Instructor

Meals In Minutes
P.O. Box 1828 • Edmond, OK 73083
Order Line: 1-800-580-1414

Voice: (405) 341-4545
Fax: (405) 348-3741
E-mail: jayne@healthfulfood.com

www.healthfulfood.com

VALUABLE RESOURCES

ARROWHEAD MILLS

Most all health food stores carry this company's quality products. For more information, visit your local health food store or call Arrowhead Mills: 1-800-749-0730

BOB'S RED MILL

Most all health food stores carry this company's qualtiy products. They provide mail order for all products including bulk grains, stone ground whole grain flours, beans, bean flours, etc. For information, contact Bob's Red Mill, 5209 SE International Way, Milwaukie, OR 97222, or call (503) 654-3215; or on the web, www.bobsredmill.com.

COUNTRY STORE

This company provides a wide variety of canned storage foods, cooking equipment, books, videos, and much more. They also distribute the wheat free sprouting mix I formulated called, **Nature's Best, "Balance Blend"**. For a free catalog, write or call: Country Store, 11013 NE 39th, Suite A, Vancouver, WA 98662; or call 1-888-311-8940.

PRO VISION FARMS

ProVision's mission is to help encourage the use, and provide a quality supply, of minimally processed food products, i.e.; whole red wheat berries, cracked red wheat, rolled white wheat flakes, stone ground whole red wheat flour, long grain brown rice, corn meal, pearled barley, rolled oat flakes, whole and dehydrated beans, all types of bean and lentil flour, milk and cheese powder, and much more. An introduction to "natural food" cooking can be simplified by use of ProVision's "Natural Food Sampler" packages containing how-to books. For more information contact: ProVision Farms, 303 S. Main St., Crookston, MN 56716; Toll Free, 1-877-776-3276; E-Mail, food@means.net; or on the web, www.provisionfarms.com.

READY FOODS 2000

Ready Foods 2000 is one of three companies nationally that sells a full line of sprouting seeds to the commercial sprouting industry. They have customers worldwide. All of their sprouting seeds are untreated, they are sprout-industry approved, and where recommended by FDA/USDA, they are tested negative for salmonella and e.coli. Their excellent sprouting seeds are used in my Nature's Best sprouting mix which is available from Country Store. (See above.) For more information about Ready Foods 2000, contact them at 7300 NW Expressway, Suite 126, Oklahoma City, OK 73132; Fax (405) 373-2853; E-mail, readyfood@aol.com; or on the web, www.readyfoods2000.com.

OTHER VALUABLE BOOKS, TAPES, & VIDEOS

THE FOOD STORAGE BIBLE
by Jayne Benkendorf $16.95

Before making another trip to the grocery store, read this book! Over 5000 products listed - by brand name - that are free of harmful additives and preservatives. Each product is coded for fat, sodium, sugar, cholesterol and over-processing.

• Quick, easy **reference guide** to help you choose the best foods.

• Learn foods to limit and those to avoid to help you **feel better fast.**

• Take an active role in using and storing foods to help you **maintain good health.** Order Line: 1-800-580-1414.

15 MINUTE STORAGE MEALS
by Jayne Benkendorf $12.95

Quick, Healthful Recipes & Food Storage Handbook

Learn to choose the best products from your grocery store to stock a Healthy Pantry.

• HOW MUCH TO STORE for 1 month **using recipes from this book!**
• HIGH ENERGY MEALS in 15 minutes - or less!
• NO ADDITIVES OR PRESERVATIVES - for better health.
• SPROUTING - for beginners.

Order line: 1-800-580-1414

NEVER GO HUNGRY, audio cassette
by Jayne Benkendorf. $6.95

This tape tells why diets don't work, and
instructs the listener how to make simple
lifestyle changes for optimum health and
weight control. Order Line: 1-800-580-1414

EATING IN RESTAURANTS, audio cassette
by Jayne Benkendorf.   *$6.95*

This tape tells how to order and what to order
for good health when eating in restaurants.
Order Line: 1-800-580-1414

THE NEW PASSPORT TO SURVIVAL
by Rita Bingham $15.95

12 Steps to Self-Sufficient Living. Learn how
to afford and maintain a year's supply, how
to build your preparedness library, and: What
to Store & Where, Storing & Treating Water,
What Foods to Eat & Why, Food Preparation
Equipment, Tasty Whole Food Recipes,
Emergency Doctorin', and much more.

Order Line: 1-888-232-6706

COUNTRY BEANS,
by Rita Bingham. $14.95

Nearly 400 quick, easy, meatless bean recipes
with over 110 bean flour recipes, including
FAST, fat-free 3-minute bean soups and 5-
minute bean dips. Most recipes are wheat-
free, gluten-free, and dairy-free.

Order Line: 1-888-232-6706

NATURAL MEALS IN MINUTES
by Rita Bingham. $14.95

Over 300 quick, high-fiber, low-fat, meatless recipes using basic foods...Grains, Legumes, Vegetables, and Fruits; Powdered Milk Cheeses in 3 minutes; Sprouting. Learn to cook grains in 15 minutes. Order Line: 1-888-232-6706

1-2-3 SMOOTHIES
by Rita Bingham $14.95

123 quick, frosty drinks. Make your own "milk" from stored grains. Delicious, nutritious meal-in-a-glass smoothies made with 100% natural ingredients. No sugar or preservatives. Recipes so easy children can blend their own tasty treats. Order Line: 1-888-232-6706

FOOD COMBINING HANDBOOK
by Rita Bingham $7.95

Learn how to combine the best foods on earth - Fruits, Vegetables, Grains, Legumes, Nuts and Seeds - for best digestion, increased energy and improved health. Order Line: 1-888-232-6706

QUICK WHOLESOME FOODS
video with recipe booklet
by Rita Bingham and LeArta Moulton. $29.95

65 minute VHS covers breads, gluten, grains, non-fat cheeses, yogurt, sprouting, and beans. Order Line: 1-888-232-6706

The Amazing WHEAT BOOK
by LeArta Moulton. $15.95

Meatless recipes using gluten made from whole wheat flour or commercial gluten flour. Over 500 great breads, seasonings, crackers, and desserts. Order Line: 1-888-554-3727 (Note: Some recipes contain refined sugar.)

INDEX

164

MEALS IN MINUTES
P.O. Box 1828 • Edmond, OK 73083
Order Line: 1-800-580-1414

Voice: (405) 341-4545
Fax: (405) 348-3741
e-mail: jayne@healthfulfood.com

www.healthfulfood.com